The Bedtime Book of Animals

Take a peek at more than **100** of your favourite animals

Written by: Zeshan Akhter
Illustrated by: Jean Claude, Livi Gosling, Kaja Kajfez, Charlotte Milner, Marc Pattenden, Sandhya Prabhat, Kate Slater, Sara Ugolotti

Contents

Tree of life	4
Habitats	6
Food chains	8

Mammals

Big cats	12
More big cats	14
Cat	16
Dog	18
Wolf	20
Fox & Dingo	21
Sea otter	22
Badger & Skunk	23
Walrus	24
Seal	25
Brown bear	26
Polar bear	27
Giant panda	28
Red panda	29
Rhinoceros	30
Horse	32
Zebra	33
Yak	34
Deer & Moose	35
Buffalo	36
Cow & Sheep	37
Camel	38
Giraffe	39
Alpaca	40
Vicuña & Llama	41
Whale	42
Dolphin	44
Narwhal	45
Hippopotamus	46
Bat	48
Hedgehog	50
Mole	51
Rabbit	52
Hare	53
Rodents	54
Gorilla	56
Orangutan	57
Monkey	58
Sloth	60
Armadillo & Anteater	61
Elephant	62
Marsupials	64
Platypus	66
Echidna	67

Birds

Songbirds	70
Parrot	72
Cockatoo	73
Toucan	74
Woodpecker	75
Kingfisher	76
Kookaburra	77
Birds of prey	78
Owl	80

Penguin	82
Flamingo	84
Water birds	85
Peafowl	86
Chicken	87
Kiwi	88
Ostrich	89

Reptiles

Crocodile	92
Caiman & Alligator	93
Lizard	94
Iguana	95
Chameleon	96
Snake	98
Sea turtle	100
Tortoise	101

Amphibians

Toad	104
Frog	105
Salamander	106
Newt	107

Fish

Zebrafish	110
Lionfish	111
Seahorse	112
X-ray fish	114
Piranha	115
Stingray	116
Shark	117

Invertebrates

Sea urchin	120
Starfish	121
Flying insects	122
Butterfly	124
Dragonfly	125
Beetle	126
Ladybird	127
Scorpion	128
Spider	129
Crab	130
Mantis shrimp & Krill	131
Octopus	132
Cuttlefish & Nautilus	133
Snail & Slug	134
Mussel & Nudibranch	135
Jellyfish & Sea pen	136
Anemone & Coral	137
Extinct	138
Endangered	139
Glossary	140
Animal A–Z	142
Acknowledgements	144

Mammals

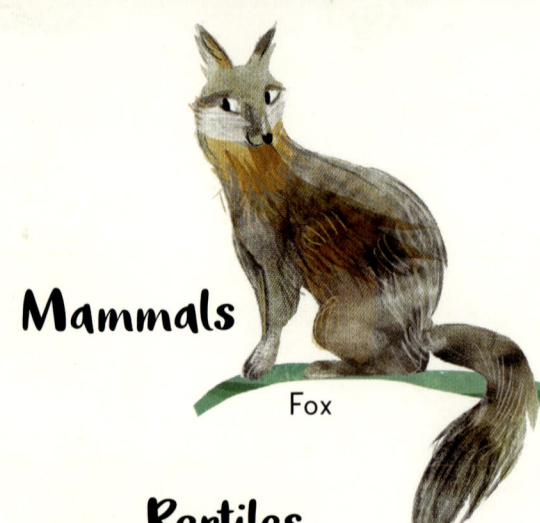
Fox

Mammals have either **fur** or **hair**. Babies drink their mother's **milk**.

Reptiles

Snake

Reptiles have **scales** or hard **plates** on their bodies. Most lay **eggs**.

Fish

Shark

Fish live in water and have **gills**. Most have **scales** and **fins**.

Tree of life

The tree of life shows how all living things are **related** to each other. It puts animals that are like one another into different groups.

Birds

Birds have two **wings**, a **beak**, and two **clawed feet**.

Parrot

Amphibians

Amphibians have **smooth skin** with no scales, hair, or feathers.

Frog

Invertebrates

Jellyfish

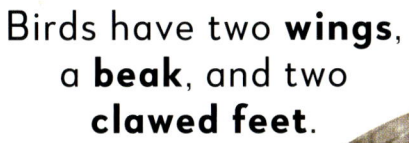

Invertebrates **do not have skeletons** inside their bodies.

Bee

All animals that are not invertebrates are **vertebrates**. This means that they have a **backbone**.

9 out of 10 animals are invertebrates.

Habitats

Habitats are places where animals live. There are many different habitats all over the world. An animal's habitat is the **best place** for it.

Mountain
Some animals live high in the mountains, often in harsh weather.

Forest
These tree-filled places can be woodlands or rainforests.

Polar

Polar habitats are cold, snowy, and surrounded by icy seas.

Ocean

Oceans are huge areas of salty water that cover much of our planet.

Grassland

These wide-open spaces are covered by grass and sometimes flowers.

Desert

Deserts are hot or cold places where not much rain falls.

Food chains

A food chain is the story of how living things get **energy** from the food they eat. Whether eating or being eaten, all animals are part of a food chain.

Grass

Wildebeest

A producer **makes its own food** using sunlight and water.

Primary consumers cannot make their own food. They eat **plants**.

Animal diets

There are three main groups of animals based on their diet. Carnivores eat meat, herbivores eat plants, and omnivores eat both.

Carnivore

Herbivore

Omnivore

Secondary consumer

Lion

These **predators** catch and eat primary consumers as **prey**.

Decomposer

Dung beetle

Decomposers eat animal **poo** and **dead** plants and animals.

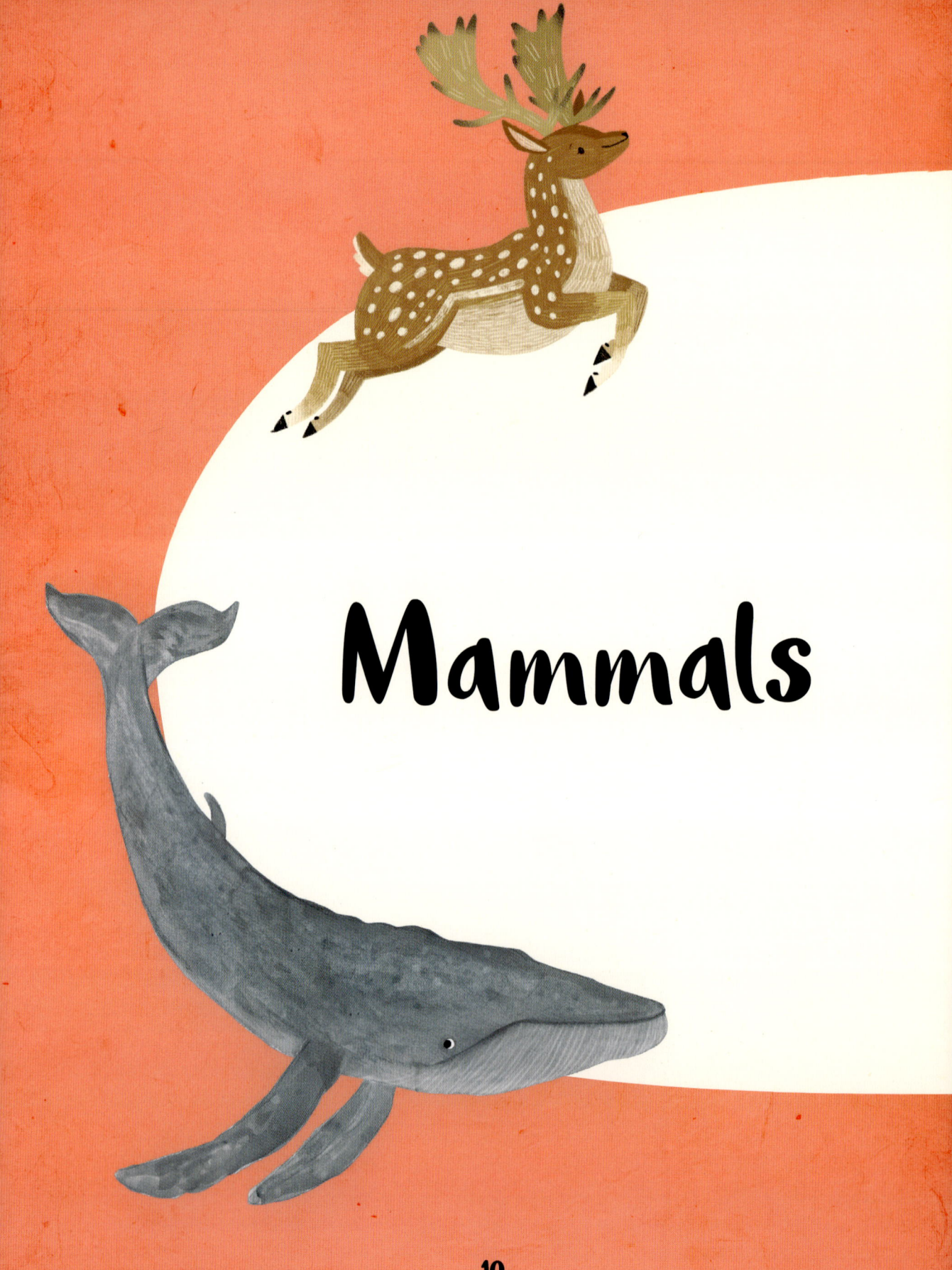

Mammals

From mini mice to whopping whales, mammals can be found roaming the land or swimming in the seas. All mammals have hair, whether it's a little or a lot!

Mammals

Big cats

These are no ordinary cats. They are much larger, and they are also some of the **fastest** and **strongest** animals in the world.

Stripy fur

Tigers are the **largest** and **strongest** of all cats.

Each **paw** has sharp **claws**.

Tiger

Grown-up male lions have a thick, shaggy **mane**.

Lions live in groups called **prides**.

Lions sleep up to 20 hours a day.

Lion

Stubby tail

Pointy ears

The bobcat can **climb** trees.

Bobcat

The spotty **cheetah** is the fastest animal on Earth. It can run three times faster than any human.

Cheetah

Strong legs

This big cat can live in jungles and deserts.

Some big cats **roar** to scare enemies away. Other cats can only purr instead.

Puma

Mammals

More big cats

Most big cats usually live **alone**, except mothers looking after their **cubs**.

Leopard spots are called **rosettes**.

Spotty fur helps leopards to hide in the grass.

Leopard

Whiskers

Snow leopard

The **stealthy** snow leopard is known as the "ghost of the mountains".

Snow leopards live on cold mountain slopes.

Jaguars can be spotty or plain black.

Jaguar

Climbing trees helps jaguars find prey.

Big cats have excellent **eyesight** and can move very **quietly**. They often hunt at night, when they can sneak up on prey and pounce.

Big cats like to stretch, especially after sleeping.

Black panther

Big, sharp teeth

Mammals

Cat

Black or white, spotty or striped, there are many types of small cat. These adorable animals make good **pets**, because they can be soft, cuddly, and playful.

Most cats have 12 **whiskers** on each cheek.

Spotty coat

Bengal cat

Stripy fur

Cat **paws** are very sensitive. They can feel tiny objects.

Tabby cat

Cats have sharp **hearing** and especially excellent **eyesight**. They can see very well in the dark.

Glossy black coat

Bombay cat

Pale fur coat
Dark tail

Siamese cat

Long white hair
Bushy tail

Persian cat

Short, thick fur

British shorthair cat

Cats purr when they are feeling happy and calm.
Meow!

Mammals

Dog

Labrador — Golden fur

Sheepdog — Long, thick coat for warmth

Dachshund — Long, narrow body; Short legs

Dogs of all shapes and sizes love going for **walks**, eating treats, playing with toys, and being stroked.

Many dogs can make wonderful pets because they are friendly and cuddly. They are very **loyal** animals.

Soft, fluffy fur

Collie

White fur with black spots

Dalmatian

Greyhounds are the **fastest** dogs in the world.

Slender body

Greyhound

These clever creatures talk to each other by **barking**. Woof woof!

Mammals

Wolf

Wolves live in groups called packs. They **howl** to talk to one another. These eery calls are very loud, so they can be heard a long way away.

Hooowl!

Wolves often hunt at **night**.

Wolves have **two layers** of fur to keep them warm.

White fur helps the Arctic wolf stay hidden in the snow.

Fox

The **Fennec fox** is very small, but has large ears.

Most foxes have long, bushy tails.

Foxes hunt for food at night. They have fantastic **hearing**, sharp eyesight, and a super sense of smell.

Dingo

Dingoes are dog-like animals that live in many parts of Australia. They are fast runners, **high jumpers**, and brilliant diggers.

Pointy ears

Dingoes can leap up more than twice their own height!

White paws

Mammals

Thick, waterproof fur keeps sea otters warm.

Sea otters dive deep underwater to find food to eat.

Sea otter

These furry swimmers live in the ocean. They like to **float** on their back and nap in the sun. Sometimes, they **smash** shells with rocks to get at the food inside.

Sea otters love to munch on sea urchins.

Badger

Badgers burrow underground to dig out dens, called **setts**. They put grass in these homes to make them cosy.

Badgers can't see very well, so they use their **ears** and **nose** to find their way around.

Sniff, sniff, snuffle

Watch out! Skunks can **squirt** a smelly liquid from their bottom.

Skunk

Stripy skunks eat almost **anything**. They'll even root around in rubbish to find food.

Mammals

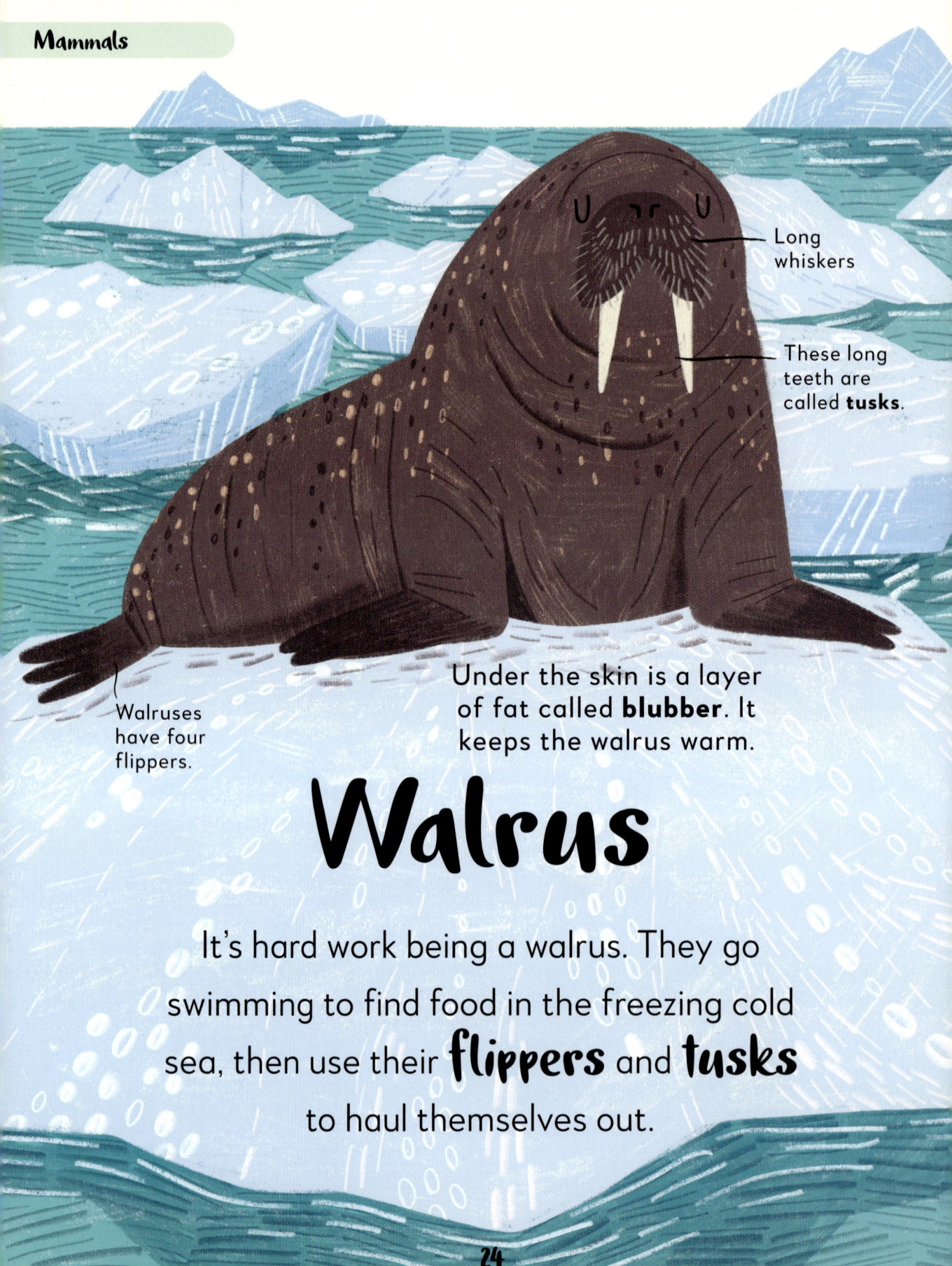

Long whiskers

These long teeth are called **tusks**.

Walruses have four flippers.

Under the skin is a layer of fat called **blubber**. It keeps the walrus warm.

Walrus

It's hard work being a walrus. They go swimming to find food in the freezing cold sea, then use their **flippers** and **tusks** to haul themselves out.

Seal

Thick fur keeps seals warm.

Seals dive deep into the icy water, looking for fish to eat. It's a good job they can hold their breath for up to half an hour!

When they're not swimming, they like lying on rocks and basking in the sun.

Whiskers help animals to sense what is around them.

Mammals

Brown bear

Brown bears sleep through the winter, snuggling up in warm, cosy dens. This is called **hibernation**. When they wake up, they feast on plants and fish.

Round ears

Black nose

Thick fur keeps brown bears warm all year round.

Brown bears use their claws to dig dens.

Sharp **claws** on each paw

Fur blends in with the white snow.

Claws help polar bears grip slippery ice and catch seals.

A baby polar bear is called a **cub**.

Polar bear

These huge beasts live near icy seas in the **freezing** far north of our planet called the Arctic. Underneath their dazzling fur, the skin is black.

Mammals

Giant panda

The giant panda's favourite food is **bamboo**, so of course they choose to live in bamboo forests! These chunky **bears** eat it almost all day long.

Chomp, chomp

Round, black ears

Black rings around eyes

Sharp teeth cut through tough bamboo.

Claws

Red pandas live in forests high up in the mountains.

Red panda

Red pandas spend most of their time in trees. They use their long, stripy tails to **balance** while scurrying around on branches.

Mammals

Rhinoceros

Rhinoceroses, or rhinos for short, live in hot places. They cool off by wallowing in **mud baths**. The mud stops their skin from burning in the Sun.

Thick, grey skin

Rhinos are very big and powerful, and they can get quite angry. When they fight, they use their **nose horn** as a weapon.

Rhinos are the second largest land animals.

A baby rhino is called a **calf**.

Rhinos only eat grass and other plants.

Mammals

Horse

Horses are strong, powerful, and can run at great speeds. Each one has a hairy **mane**, a long **tail**, and hard **hooves** on its feet.

The **mane** grows on the top of the neck.

Small horses like this one are called **ponies**.

Shetland pony

Hoof

Horses swish their **tail** to swat away insects.

Horses can **walk** slowly, **trot** a little faster, **canter** briskly, or **gallop** at full speed.

Horse

Zebra

At first glance, horse-like zebras might all look the same, but each one has its own unique pattern of black and white **stripes** on its fur.

Zebras like to eat **grass**.

Hoof

Strong, sturdy body

Short, tufted tail

Zebras graze and play under the hot sun in Africa.

Mammals

Yak

Yaks live high up in cold mountains where there is not much air. They have big **lungs** that help them breathe. Yaks love to eat grass. They travel great distances to find it.

A woolly, waterproof coat keeps yaks warm and dry.

Long horns

Long tail

Hooves

Yaks use their horns to move snow to look for food.

Deer

Deer roam woodlands to find leaves, shrubs, and grasses to eat. Male deer have **antlers**, which fall off in winter but grow back again each spring.

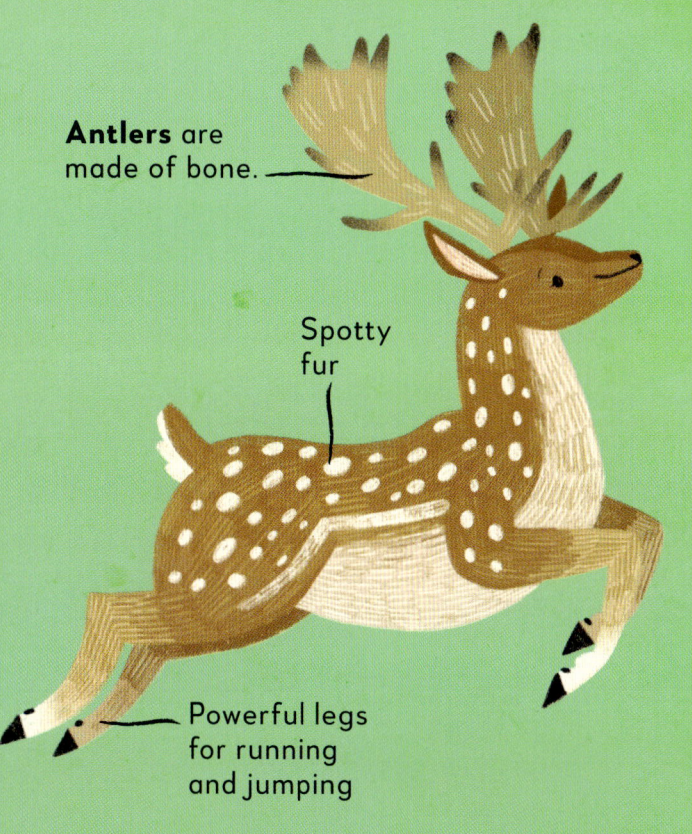

Antlers are made of bone.

Spotty fur

Powerful legs for running and jumping

Large antlers **impress** other deer.

Moose

Short tail

Hefty, hairy moose are the **largest** type of deer. Surprisingly, they can swim!

This flap of hairy skin is called a **dewlap**.

Thick body hair

35

Mammals

Buffalo

There can be **thousands** of sturdy buffalo in a single herd. Their strength in numbers helps to keep them safe from unfriendly animals!

A buffalo's horns grow right across its head.

Curved horns

Droopy ears

Cow

Straight back

Cows are **calm**, sturdy animals. They often live in groups and spend most of their time eating grass.

Moo!

A cow's stomach has **four** sections that help break down food.

Udders make milk to feed baby cows, or calves.

Thick, curly **fleece**

Baa!

Sheep

These woolly bundles are often found grazing in fields. They live in groups called **flocks**.

Mammals

Camel

The **hump** stores fat that the camel can live off for weeks.

Two layers of long **eyelashes** keep out sand and dust.

A camel can drink a whole **bathtub** of water in one go!

Camels live in hot, dry **deserts**. Luckily, they can last a long time between drinks. Their long, knobbly legs are very strong.

A giraffe's tongue is dark and **sticky**.

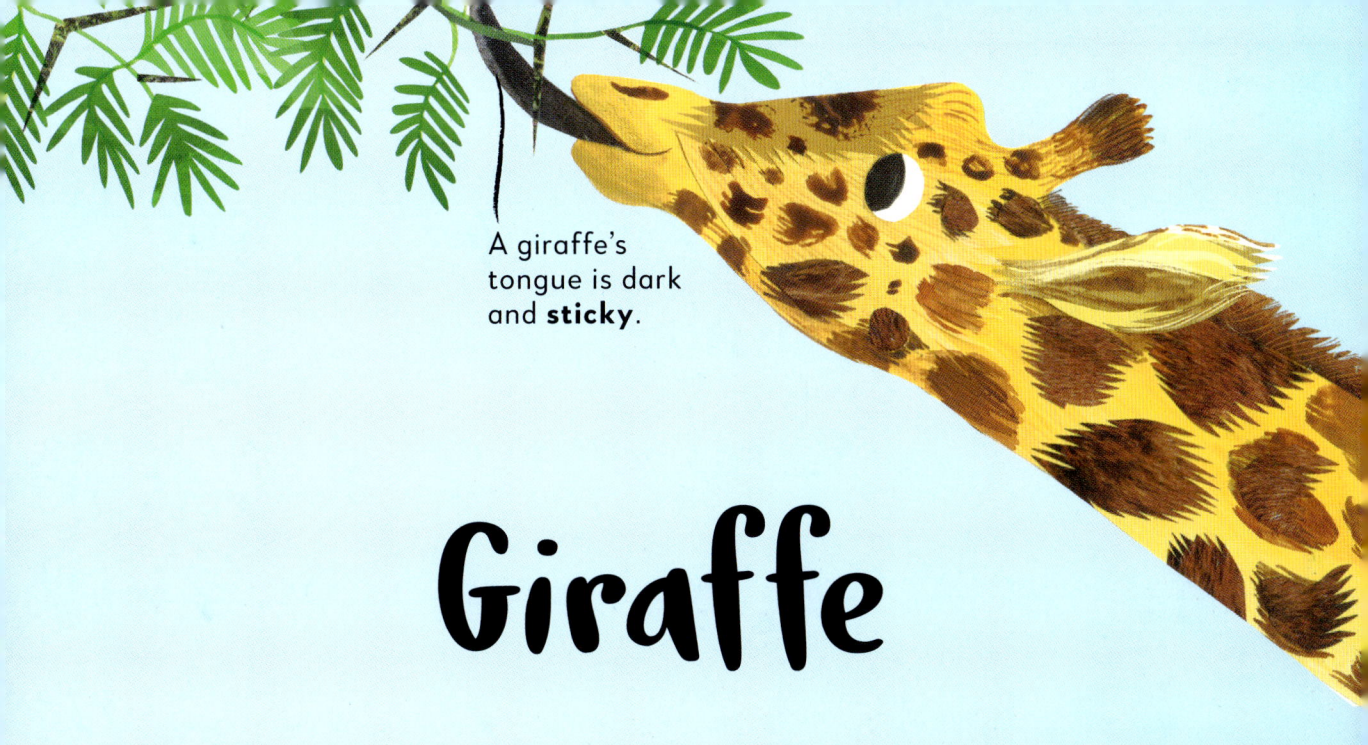

Giraffe

Giraffes are the **tallest** animals in the whole wide world. Some are taller than a house! They live in Africa.

These bony points are called **ossicones**.

Golden fur with large brown patches

Having such a **long** neck is useful for reaching tasty leaves high up on trees.

Mammals

Alpaca

Alpacas, vicuñas, and llamas all live in the mountains of **South America**.

Alpaca hair can be made into woolly jumpers.

Alpacas mostly eat grass.

Stocky body shape

Alpacas do not live in the wild. They are looked after by farmers and live together in groups called **herds**. They look cuddly, but watch out for their kick!

Vicuña

Vicuñas roam free high up on the mountainside. They are fast runners with fine, soft fur.

Slender legs

Long, curvy ears

Llama

Llamas are strong and can balance on steep hills. In their rocky homelands, they often help people carry things.

Mammals

Whale

These mighty sea creatures are record-breaking **divers**. Some whales can hold their breath for up to an hour!

Smooth skin

These strips, called **baleen**, help this whale to filter food from the sea.

Grey whale

Blue whale

Whales talk using clicks, whistles, and musical calls.

Long **flippers** for speedy swimming

Humpback whale

42

Minke whale

White belly

Swishing tail fins power whales through the water.

Whales live in groups called pods.

The blue whale is the **largest** animal on Earth. It is as long as an aeroplane!

Whales come to the surface to breathe through **blowholes** on their backs.

The **dorsal fin** is on the whale's back. It helps with balance.

Sperm whale

Small, beady eyes

Mammals

Dolphins are very fast swimmers.

Dolphins breathe through their **blowhole**.

Tail fin, called a **fluke**

Flipper

Common dolphin

Dolphin

Dolphins are clever and playful. They travel together in **pods**, talk to each other in clicks and whistles, and like to leap out of the sea.

Dorsal fin for balance

The orca is the **largest** dolphin. It can weigh more than three cars!

Smooth skin

Orca

Narwhal

Narwhals live in freezing seawater surrounded by ice. The long spike on their head is called a **tusk**, which is a type of tooth.

A narwhal's **tusk** can grow to be longer than a grown-up human!

Tail fin

Narwhals are nicknamed "unicorns of the sea."

Mammals

Hippopotamus

Hefty hippopotamuses spend most of their day relaxing in water. This keeps them cool in the **heat**, as it is very warm in their grassland homes.

Thick skin

These plant-eaters love to eat grass.

Grunt grunt!

Honk honk!

Hippos are very **protective** of their families. They will use their teeth as a weapon if they are in danger.

A group of hippopotamuses is called a bloat.

A hippopotamus has almost **no hair** on its body.

A baby hippopotamus is called a calf.

Huge teeth look a bit like tusks.

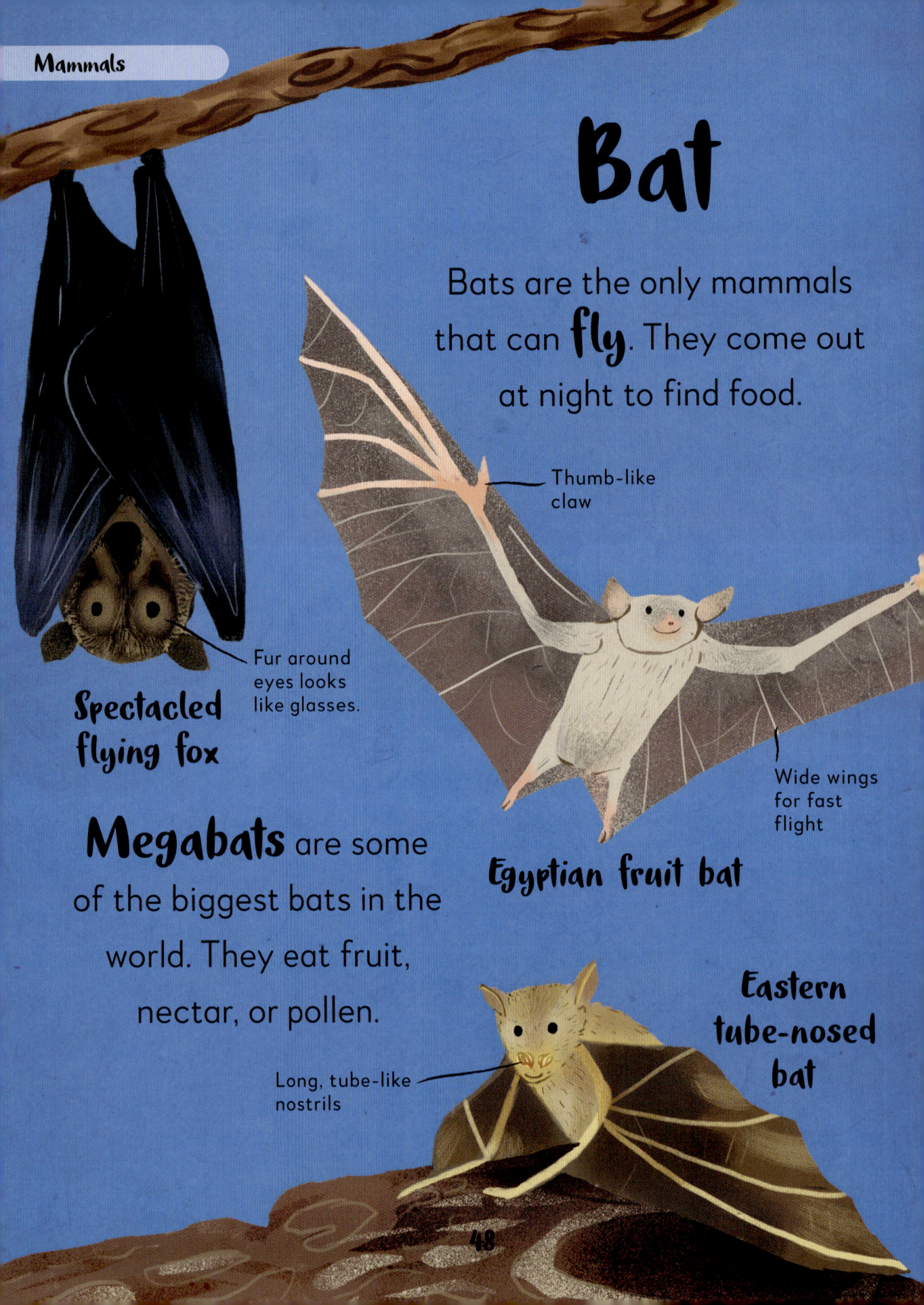

Mammals

Bat

Bats are the only mammals that can **fly**. They come out at night to find food.

Thumb-like claw

Fur around eyes looks like glasses.

Spectacled flying fox

Megabats are some of the biggest bats in the world. They eat fruit, nectar, or pollen.

Wide wings for fast flight

Egyptian fruit bat

Long, tube-like nostrils

Eastern tube-nosed bat

48

Many bats use sound to find their food. This is called echolocation.

- Wide wings
- Fluffy, brown body fur

Daubenton's bat

Some of the smallest bats in the world are **microbats**. They mostly eat insects.

- Yellow wings
- Grey fur on body

Yellow-winged bat

- Two huge ears
- This is called a noseleaf.

Sword-nosed bat

Mammals

Hedgehog

A hedgehog curls up into a ball if it is scared.

Hedgehogs are small, spiky animals. They **sleep** during the day and come out at night to find food.

Pointy spikes, called **quills**

Long **snout** for sniffing out food

Hedgehogs like to eat **berries**, but look for beetles and caterpillars to chomp on too.

Paws with long, sharp claws

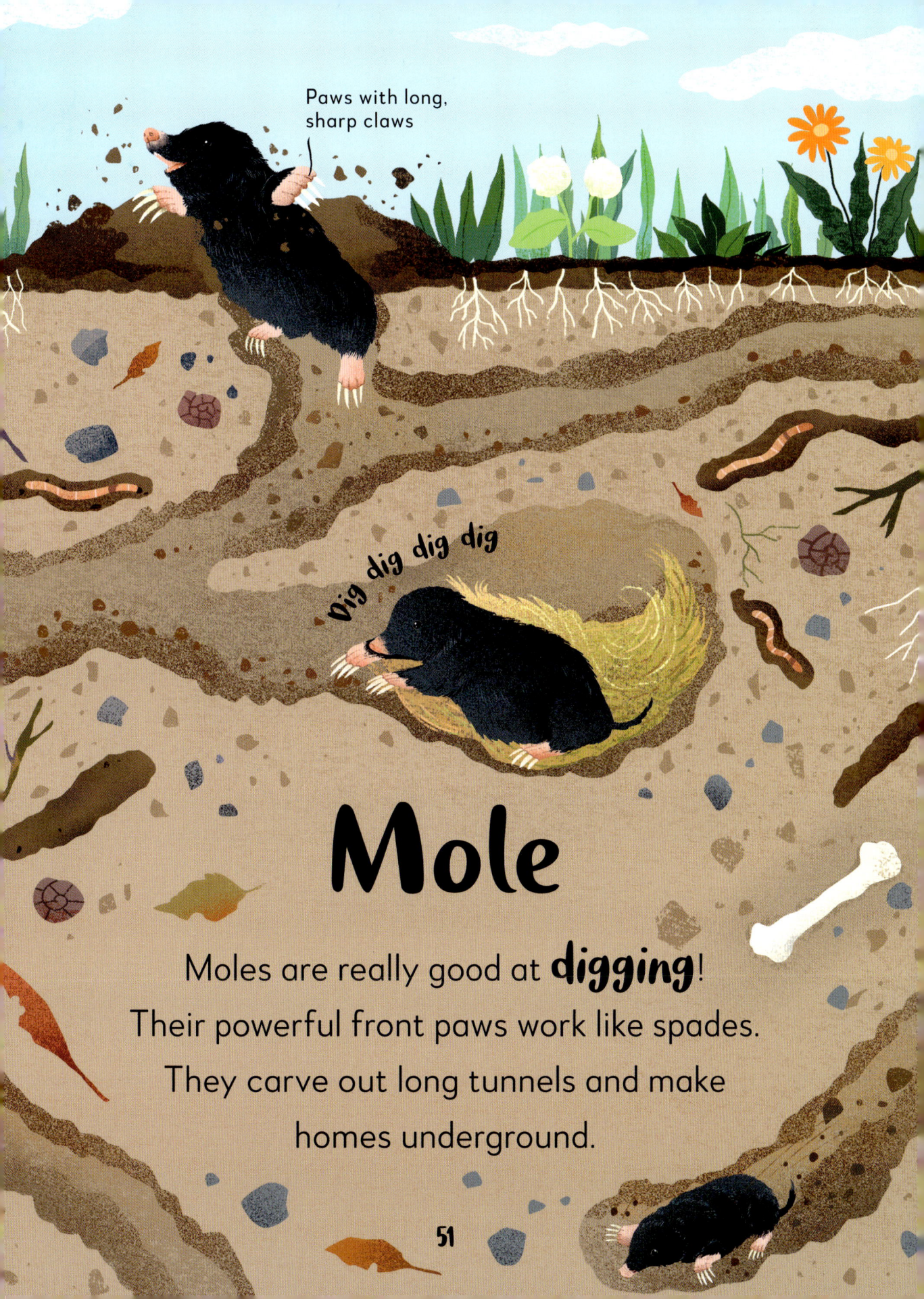

Dig dig dig dig

Mole

Moles are really good at **digging**! Their powerful front paws work like spades. They carve out long tunnels and make homes underground.

Mammals

Rabbit

Rabbits live in underground homes called burrows. Above ground, they **hop** from place to place, nibbling on plants as they go.

Some kinds of rabbits are sweet and cuddly and make excellent **pets**.

Round, fluffy tail

Soft fur

Long ears

Whiskers

Rabbits have teeth and nails that never stop growing.

Hare

Like rabbits, hares have good **hearing**.

Sometimes hares need to escape predators. Luckily, they can run extremely **fast**.

Snowshoe hare

Big feet help this hare balance on snow and ice.

Huge ears

Hares are **larger** than rabbits.

Hares have long, strong back legs, helping them to **bound** quickly across the ground.

American desert hare

Mammals

Rodents

Small, furry rodents are found almost everywhere in the world. They gnaw on food with sharp, pointy **teeth** that never stop growing!

Capybaras are the **largest** rodents. They are very friendly animals.

Capybara

Pygmy jerboa

This is the **smallest** of all rodents. It hops to move around.

Whiskers

Tiny mice can **jump**, **climb**, and even **swim**.

Mouse

54

Beavers build homes from branches, twigs, and mud.

A beaver's tail looks a little like a paddle.

Beaver

Some rodents live alone, but many live in groups. These groups have underground homes near one another called **towns**.

Guinea pigs don't have **tails**.

Guinea pig

Feet on very short legs

Mammals

Gorilla

Gorillas have thick, black hair.

Gorilla families live together in the beautiful forests of Africa.

Gorillas can feel happy and sad, just like humans.

Strong, muscly legs

Boom, boom! Gorillas **beat** their chests to show how big and strong they are, but they are gentle giants. They are quite happy eating leaves.

Orangutan

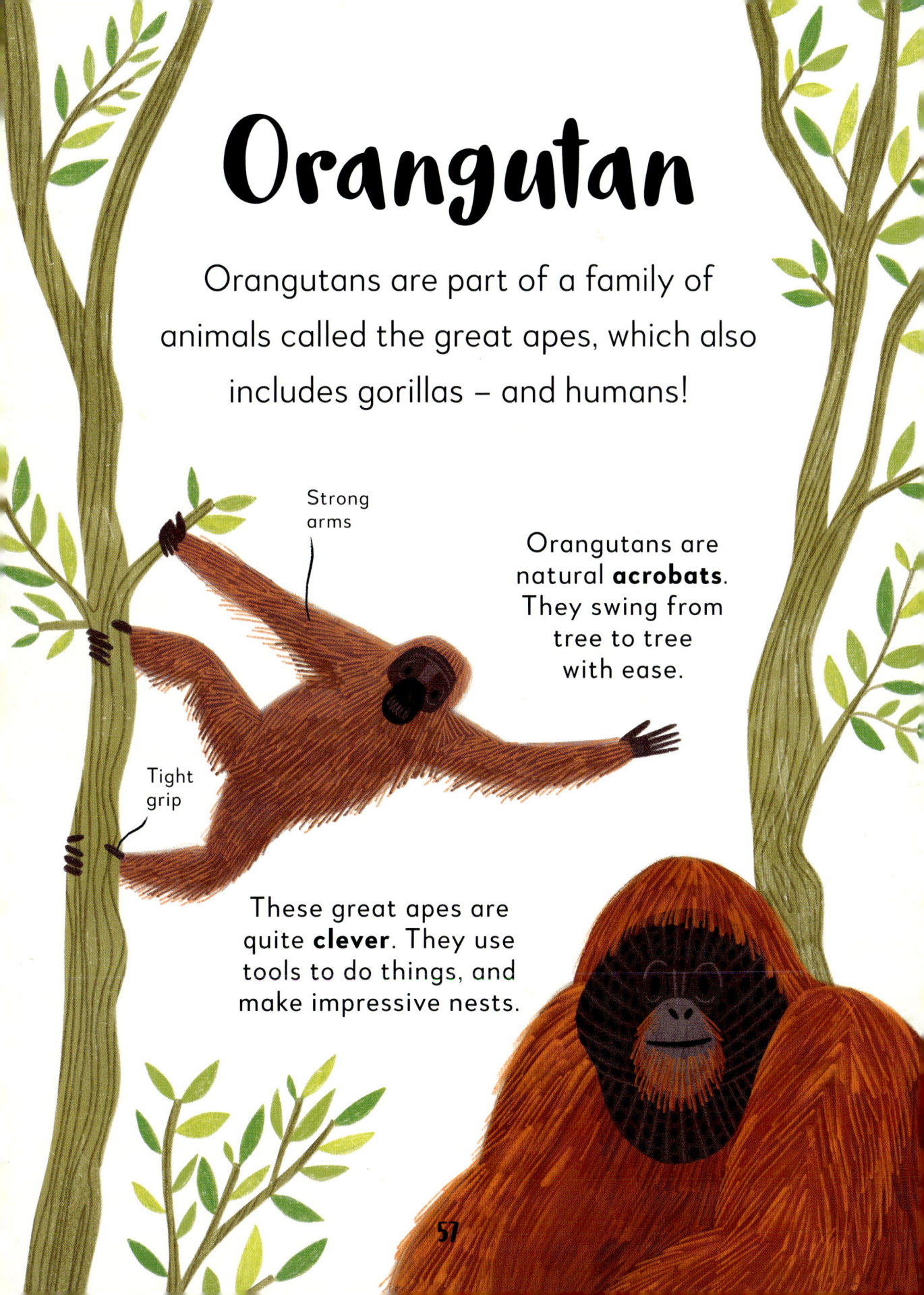

Orangutans are part of a family of animals called the great apes, which also includes gorillas – and humans!

Strong arms

Orangutans are natural **acrobats**. They swing from tree to tree with ease.

Tight grip

These great apes are quite **clever**. They use tools to do things, and make impressive nests.

Mammals

Monkey

There are hundreds of different types of monkeys that live all over the world. Monkeys can **swing** between tree branches to get from place to place.

Ooh aah aah!

Its face gets even brighter when it is **excited**.

The mandrill is the **largest** of all monkeys.

Hair grows around its colourful face, but not on it.

Mandrill

Some monkeys like to stay **high** up in trees, but others come down and scamper around on the forest floor.

Vervet monkey

Monkeys like to eat fruit, leaves, nuts, and insects. Young monkeys love to **play**!

Golden snub-nosed monkey

Monkeys live in groups called **troops**.

Golden marmoset

Mammals

Sloth

Sloths live in trees in rainforests. They eat twigs and leaves. Sloths move slowly and spend most of their day **sleeping**.

Three fingers on each hand

Long, shaggy fur

Anteaters eat thousands of insects every day!

White stripe

Thick, brown fur

Armadillo

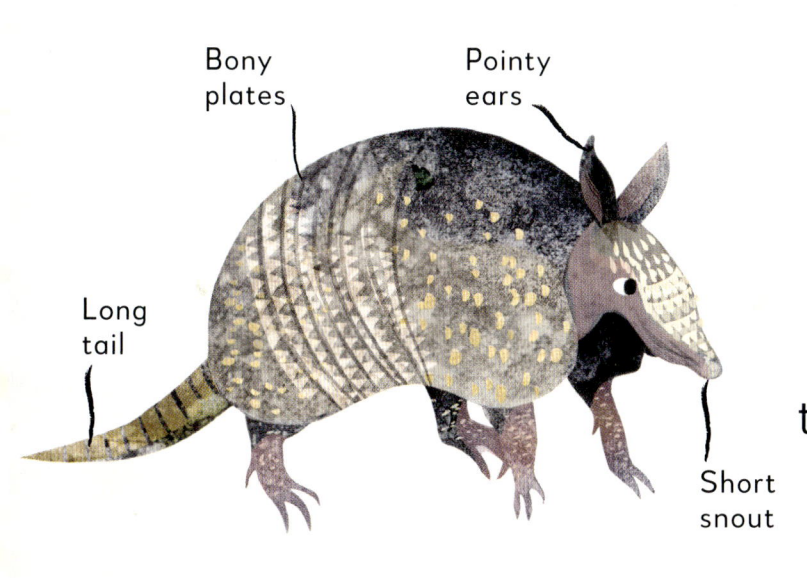

Bony plates
Pointy ears
Long tail
Short snout

Armadillos are covered in hard, bony plates. This **armour** protects them from predators.

Anteater

Thin tongue

Anteaters do not have teeth. To eat, they poke their snouts into ant nests and scoop the insects out with their **sticky** tongues.

Mammals

Elephant

Elephants can live in many different places, from lush wetlands and forests to sparse savannahs and deserts. Wherever they **roam**, elephants take great care of each other.

Big, flappy ears

Long, curved tusks

Strong legs

62

An elephant's trunk is actually a long nose. Elephants use it to smell, to grab plants to eat, and even as a **snorkel** when swimming.

Elephants live and travel in family groups called herds.

Thick, grey skin

A baby elephant is called a calf.

Mammals

Marsupials

Hairy marsupials come in many shapes and sizes. Most live in dry **deserts**, but some make their home in woodlands and rainforests.

Small, compact body shape

Whiskers

Wombat

This baby koala is nestled in its mother's pouch.

Koala

All baby marsupials are called joeys.

Strong legs for hopping around

Kangaroo

64

Opossums sometimes carry their babies on their backs.

Large, pointed ears

Wallabies look similar to kangaroos, but are smaller.

Long, furry tail

Opossum

Wallaby

Scattering of white spots on fur

Quoll

Small, round ears

A quokka is about the size of a cat.

Quokka

Mummy marsupials have a special **pouch** on their tummy. Inside, their tiny babies grow and get ready to explore.

Mammals

Platypus

A platypus has a duck-like bill and a tail like a beaver. These animals hunt for food underwater. Platypuses are one of only two mammals that **lay eggs**.

Platypuses keep their eggs safe on riverbanks by covering them with leaves and twigs.

Flipper-like feet help the platypus swim.

Thick, brown fur

Flat **bill**

Echidna

Echidnas lay eggs instead of giving birth to live young. They lay one at a time. Each echidna egg hatches into a baby called a **puggle**.

Spiky **spines** for protection

Round body

Long, thin **snout**

Sharp **claws** for digging

Birds

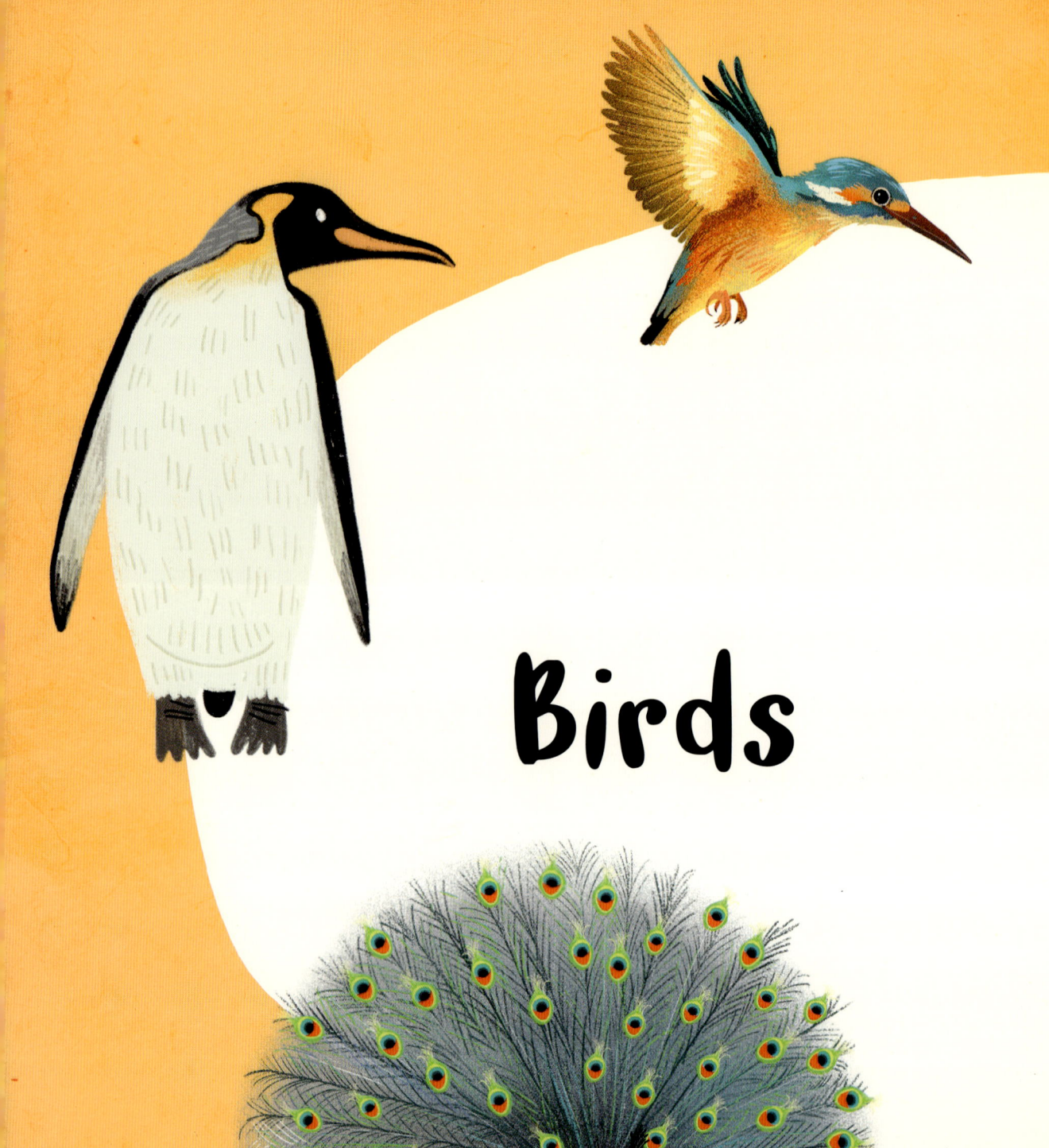

All birds have feathers and two wings, which many use to fly through the skies. These incredible creatures sing, chirp, squawk, and coo to talk to each other.

Birds

Songbirds

Thousands of birds make calls that sound **musical**. These birds are known as songbirds. They sing from dawn until dusk.

Superb starling

Red belly feathers

Painted bunting

Chirp, chirp!

Orange feathers wrap around the body.

Small, sharp beak

Northern red bishop

Blue tit

70

Songbirds can **grip** tightly onto branches. This stops them from dropping to the ground when they fall asleep.

This songbird can have a black, red, or yellow face.

Each songbird sings its own song.

Gouldian finch

Golden-fronted leafbird

This green, leaf-coloured bird blends into the trees.

Clawed feet

Blackbird

Birds

Curved beak

Sharp claws

Long tail feathers

Parrot

Parrots live in warm, tropical countries. They are clever birds and can make calls that sound like humans **speaking**!

Small head

Large wings

Parrots often have brightly coloured feathers.

Squawk!
Cockatoos make a loud, sharp screaming sound. They do this if they are bored, or to warn other cockatoos of danger.

Cockatoo

Cockatoos are a type of parrot. They are smart, playful, and **noisy**. They love spending time with other cockatoos and live together in flocks.

Yellow crest feathers

Short, sharp beak

Wings

This cockatoo is white, but others may have black, grey, or pink feathers.

Birds

Toucan

Very strong beak

Small, beady eyes

Black body feathers

Colourful toucans have enormous **beaks**, which can be longer than the rest of their bodies.

This bird hops from tree to tree, making a **croaking** noise to talk to friends.

Woodpecker

Woodpeckers use their tough beaks to **hammer** grooves into tree trunks.

Strong, sharp beak

Tap tap tap tap tap

Stiff tail feathers

They do this to build their **nests** and to find insects to eat.

Birds

Kingfisher

Whoosh!
Beautiful blue and orange kingfishers whizz down into quiet streams and rivers, catching fish to eat.

Listen out for a kingfisher's high-pitched call. **"Peep peep!"**

The pointy beak pierces the water very quickly.

Electric blue wing feathers

Stripe of grey wing feathers

Kookaburras swoop down on lizards and frogs.

Large beak

Short, brown tail feathers

Grey body

Kookaburra

You'll hear a kookaburra before you see one. They have a **noisy laugh**, but they are actually quite shy. They perch on tree branches in the forests of Australia.

Birds

Birds of prey

These awesome creatures are large, strong, and extremely fast flyers. They also have sharp claws and superb eyesight. It is no surprise, then, that they are expert **hunters**.

This is the **largest** bird of prey.

Its huge **wings** stretch out much wider than a grown-up person's arms.

Andean condor

The red kite's forked tail twists gently to keep it **balanced** in flight.

Red kite

Bald eagle

White head feathers

Bald eagles catch fish, snakes, and small mammals.

Peregrine falcon

Large eyes

When it dives through the air, the peregrine falcon travels **faster** than any other animal.

Sharp claws, called **talons**

Bald head

Vultures feed on **dead** animals.

Birds of prey **swoop** down to snatch their prey from water, the ground, or even in mid-air.

King vulture

Birds

Owl

Most of these birds of prey are **nocturnal**. This means they sleep during the day and are only awake at night-time.

Owls can fly **silently** because they have very soft feathers.

Snowy owl

Barn owl

Rounded wings

Great horned owl

Brown feathers

80

Eagle owls are the biggest owls in the world.

Small, soft feathers on the wing tip

Eagle owl

Elf owl

Huge eyes

These are not real horns! They are feathery tufts.

Short legs

Owls cannot move their eyes left or right. But they can **twist** their heads almost all the way round. This gives them a fantastic all-around view.

Birds

Penguin

Most penguins live in frozen Antarctica. They **waddle** across the ice, or slide on their bellies.

Yellow crest

The emperor penguin is the **largest** penguin in the world.

Macaroni penguin

Penguin **chicks** are covered in soft, fuzzy feathers.

Emperor penguin

82

White stripe

Black chin feathers

Chinstrap penguin

Gentoo penguin

Penguins have special wings called **flippers**. They use them to swim and dive for their favourite food: fish!

There are 18 different types of penguin.

A long, sharp **bill** is useful for catching fish.

White ring around eyes

King penguin

Adélie penguin

83

Birds

Flamingo

Curved head

Flamingos live by lakes and lagoons. They sometimes **perch** on one leg, and sleep standing up.

Pink feathers

Long neck

Thin legs

Flamingos are born grey. They eat tiny, pink-coloured shrimp, which makes their feathers **change** colour!

Webbed feet

Water birds

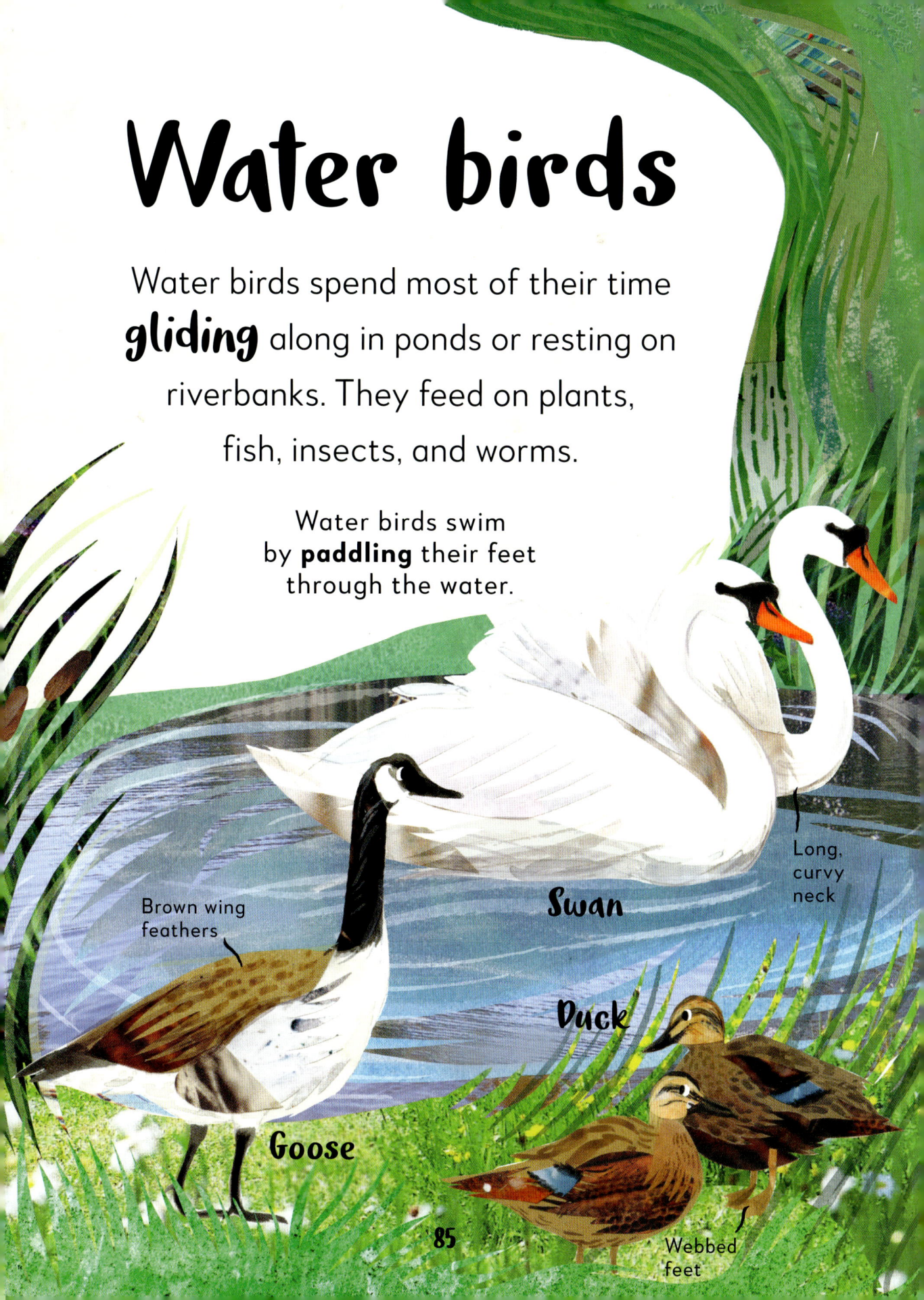

Water birds spend most of their time **gliding** along in ponds or resting on riverbanks. They feed on plants, fish, insects, and worms.

Water birds swim by **paddling** their feet through the water.

Brown wing feathers

Swan

Long, curvy neck

Duck

Goose

Webbed feet

Birds

A peacock's tail feathers are called its train.

Each feather has an **eyespot**.

Peacocks spread their feathers to attract peahens.

Peafowl

Male peafowls are called **peacocks** and female peafowls are called **peahens**. Peacocks can have up to 200 brightly coloured tail feathers, while peahens are mainly brown.

Chicken

Cluck, cluck! Many chickens live on farms. You might see them strutting around or pecking seeds and bugs from the ground.

Male chickens are called **cockerels**. They call out loudly every morning.

Cock-a-doodle-dooo!

Crest

Female chickens are called hens. They lay **eggs** that hatch into baby chicks.

Chickens have **wings**, but they're not very good at flying.

Birds

Kiwi

Kiwis have tiny wings, but they are not able to **fly**. Their wings cannot be seen through their feathers.

Hair-like feathers

Short legs

Long, thin **beak** with nostrils at the end

Kiwis walk around **sniffing** the ground. They can tell when tasty worms are wriggling underground.

Small beak

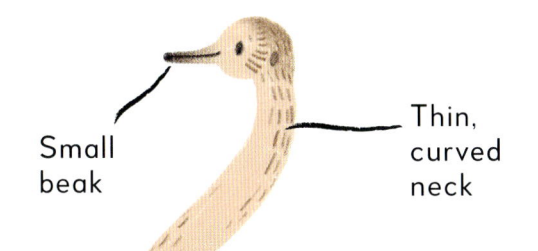

Thin, curved neck

This is the only bird with two toes on each foot.

Black and white wing feathers

Long legs

Ostrich

Ostriches live in warm deserts and savannahs. They are the biggest birds in the world. Ostriches cannot fly, but they are very fast **runners**.

Reptiles

Reptiles wriggle, slither, swim, and crawl their way across land and water. Many of these cold-blooded animals have colourful, scaly skin.

Reptiles

Crocodile

These powerful predators are the largest reptiles in the world. They can be longer than three grown-up people lying end-to-end!

V-shaped **snout**

Long, sharp **teeth**

Crocodiles have the strongest **bite** of all animals. Snap!

Crocodiles eat fish, birds, and sometimes mammals.

Caimans can see well at **night**.

Caiman

Caimans live in rivers, mangroves, swamps, lakes, and marshes. They have strong jaws with a row of **cone-shaped** teeth.

Caimans cannot chew. They **swallow** their food whole.

Alligator

Dark-coloured, scaly skin

Alligators have a U-shaped snout.

Alligators can only live in **freshwater** areas, such as rivers and swamps.

Reptiles

Lizard

Lizards are clever creatures. Some can change their skin colour, while others can remove their **tails** to escape from a predator's grasp.

Black and white neck stripes

Collared lizard

Five toes

Green **crest** on back

Green basilisk lizard

Stripy tail

Zebra-tailed lizard

Green iguana

Iguanas have **sticky tongues**, which they use to catch flies.

Curly tail

Toes with sharp **claws** for climbing

Iguana

Iguanas are a type of lizard. They love to eat insects. Some iguanas can hold their **breath** for up to half an hour when swimming!

Blue scales

Spines on back

Blue iguana

Reptiles

Chameleon

Chameleons are very colourful lizards. Most chameleons can **change** their skin **colour** to blend into their surroundings, or to show how they are feeling.

Some chameleons have **horns** to defend themselves.

If a chameleon is blue or green, it is feeling happy!

Jackson's chameleon

Pygmy chameleon

This is the **smallest** type of chameleon.

Panther chameleon

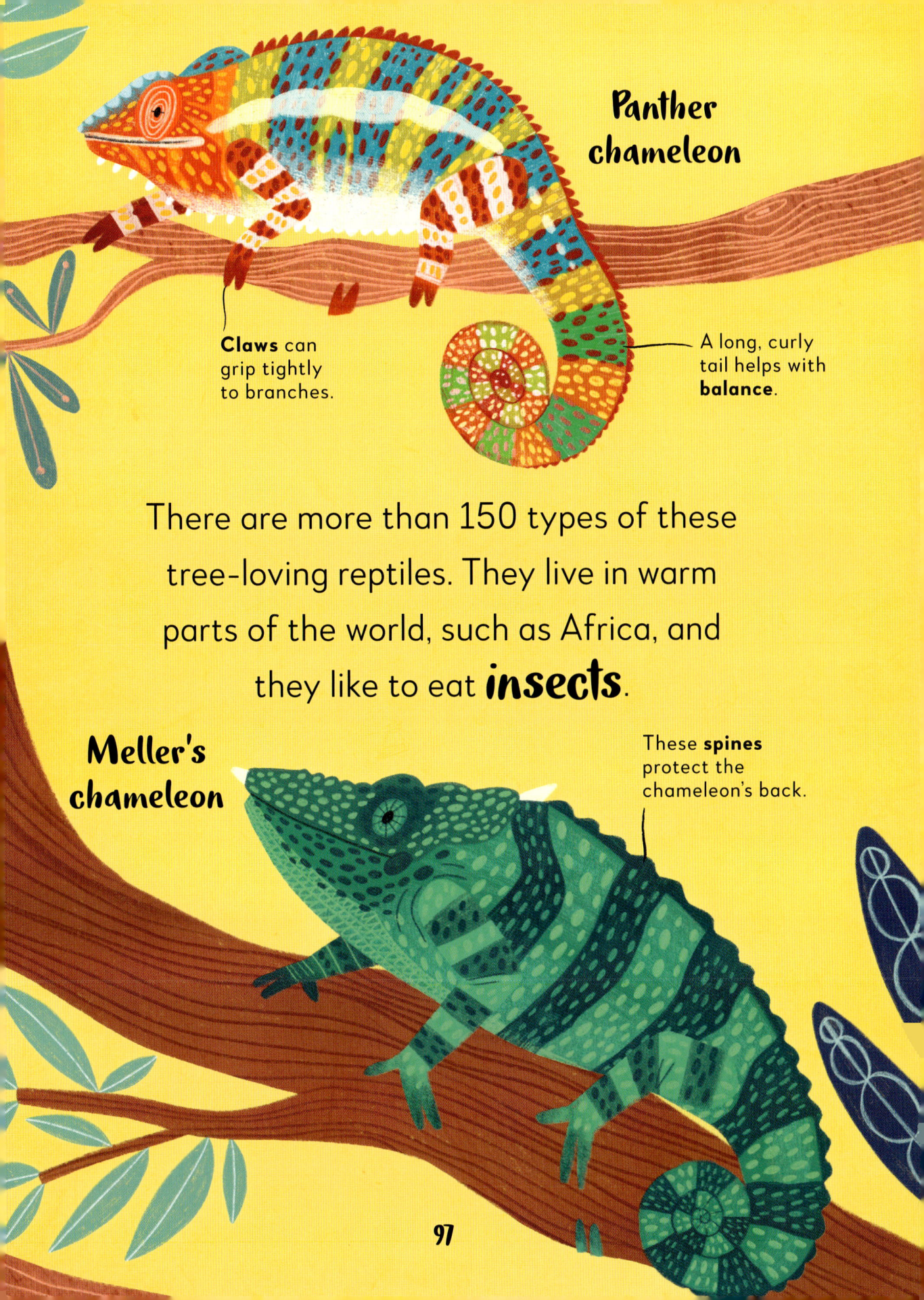

Claws can grip tightly to branches.

A long, curly tail helps with **balance**.

There are more than 150 types of these tree-loving reptiles. They live in warm parts of the world, such as Africa, and they like to eat **insects**.

Meller's chameleon

These **spines** protect the chameleon's back.

Reptiles

Snakes can wrap their bodies around tree branches.

Long green body

Stripy red and black **scales**

Honduran milk snake

Green mamba

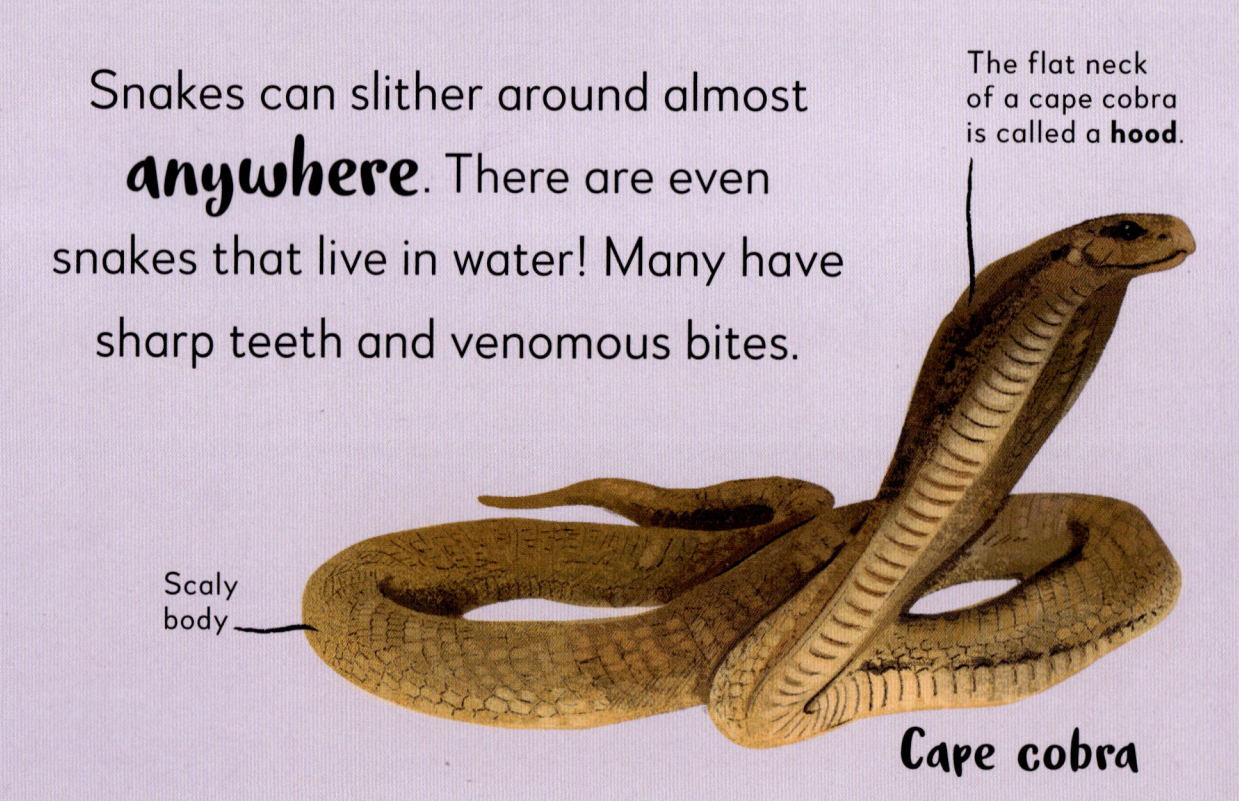

Snake

Snakes can slither around almost **anywhere**. There are even snakes that live in water! Many have sharp teeth and venomous bites.

The flat neck of a cape cobra is called a **hood**.

Scaly body

Cape cobra

Snakes like this one wrap around prey and **squeeze** it.

Small, black eyes

Red-tailed boa constrictor

Red tail

This snake's tail makes a rattling noise when it moves.

Snakes **shed** their skin many times a year. They wriggle out of their old skin, and a fresh new layer takes its place.

Timber rattlesnake

Striped body

Snakes can make a hissing sound when they breathe.

Sidewinder

Slithers sideways when moving.

Forked tongue

99

Reptiles

Sea turtle

Sea turtles spend most of their time in water and hold their **breath** when diving. Some can stay underwater for up to seven hours while they sleep!

Hard **shell**

Long **flippers**

Baby sea turtles hide in seaweed to avoid being eaten by bigger sea creatures.

Tortoises live for around 150 years.

The heavy shell is called a **carapace**.

Large neck

Clawed feet

Tortoise

Tortoises only live on land. They can pull their head and legs into their safe, strong **shell** to protect themselves from danger.

Amphibians

An amphibian's special talent is that when it is grown up, it can live on land and in water. These animals lay eggs, and many have brightly coloured skin.

Amphibians

Toad

Toads can gobble up flies, snails, and slugs with a lightning fast **flick** of the tongue. They live in damp places and **crawl** to ponds and swamps to lay eggs.

Toads make a rattling, rolling noise: "Qwarrk!"

Bumpy, dry skin

Long, sticky tongue

Croak croak!

Large eyes

Short front legs

Sticky pads on toes let tree frogs grip branches.

Tree frog

A frog **croaks** to tell other frogs where it is.

Long back legs

Wood frog

Webbed feet for swimming fast

Frog

Frogs use their long back legs to swim and **jump** around. They lay tiny eggs called frogspawn in water. The eggs hatch into babies called **tadpoles**.

Amphibians

Salamander

Some salamanders can breathe through their skin.

Webbed feet give extra grip.

This salamander can squirt **poison** from its tail!

Salamanders live in cool, wet places. They make their homes under branches, rocks, and leaves. These **slippery** creatures scamper around on all fours looking for food.

Newt

If a newt loses its leg or tail, it can regrow it!

Long, thin body

Newts are small, slimy amphibians that love to swim. Some breathe **underwater**, but others can only breathe on land.

A newt's **skin** can be smooth and wet or dry and bumpy. They like to live in ponds.

Fish

Fish make their homes underwater and use gills in order to breathe. Most fish have scales, smooth bodies, and swishing tails and fins.

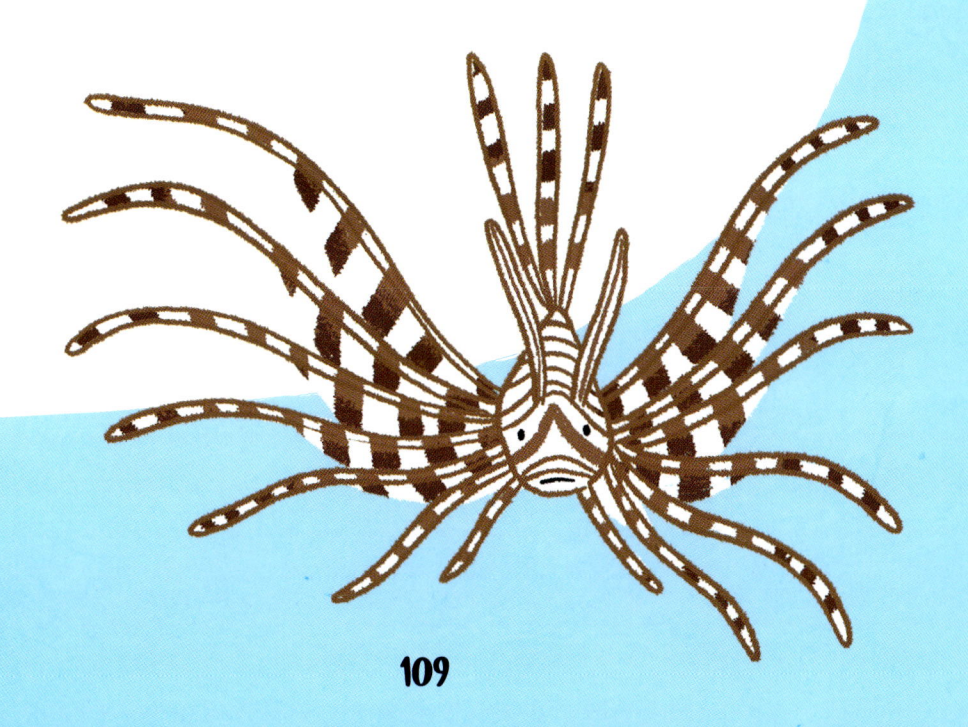

Fish

Zebrafish are usually found in ponds and lakes.

Tail fin

Five blue and white stripes

Zebrafish

These fish are named after zebras because they have similar **stripes** on their scaly skin. If they are hurt, zebrafish can regrow their skin, fins, heart, and brain.

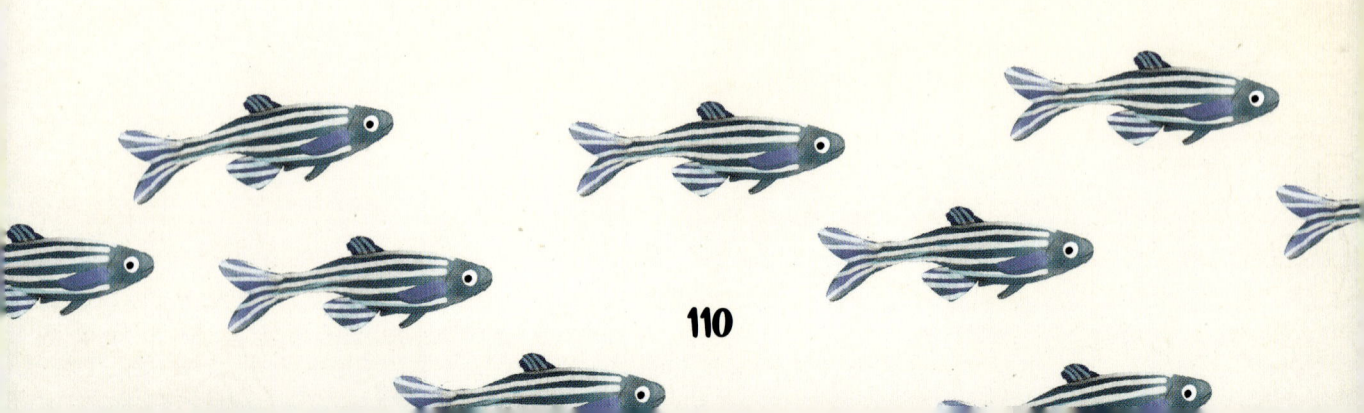

Lionfish

Lionfish live in warm waters. The **spines** on their back contain **venom**, which they use to protect themselves from predators. Lionfish are nocturnal, so they are only awake at night-time.

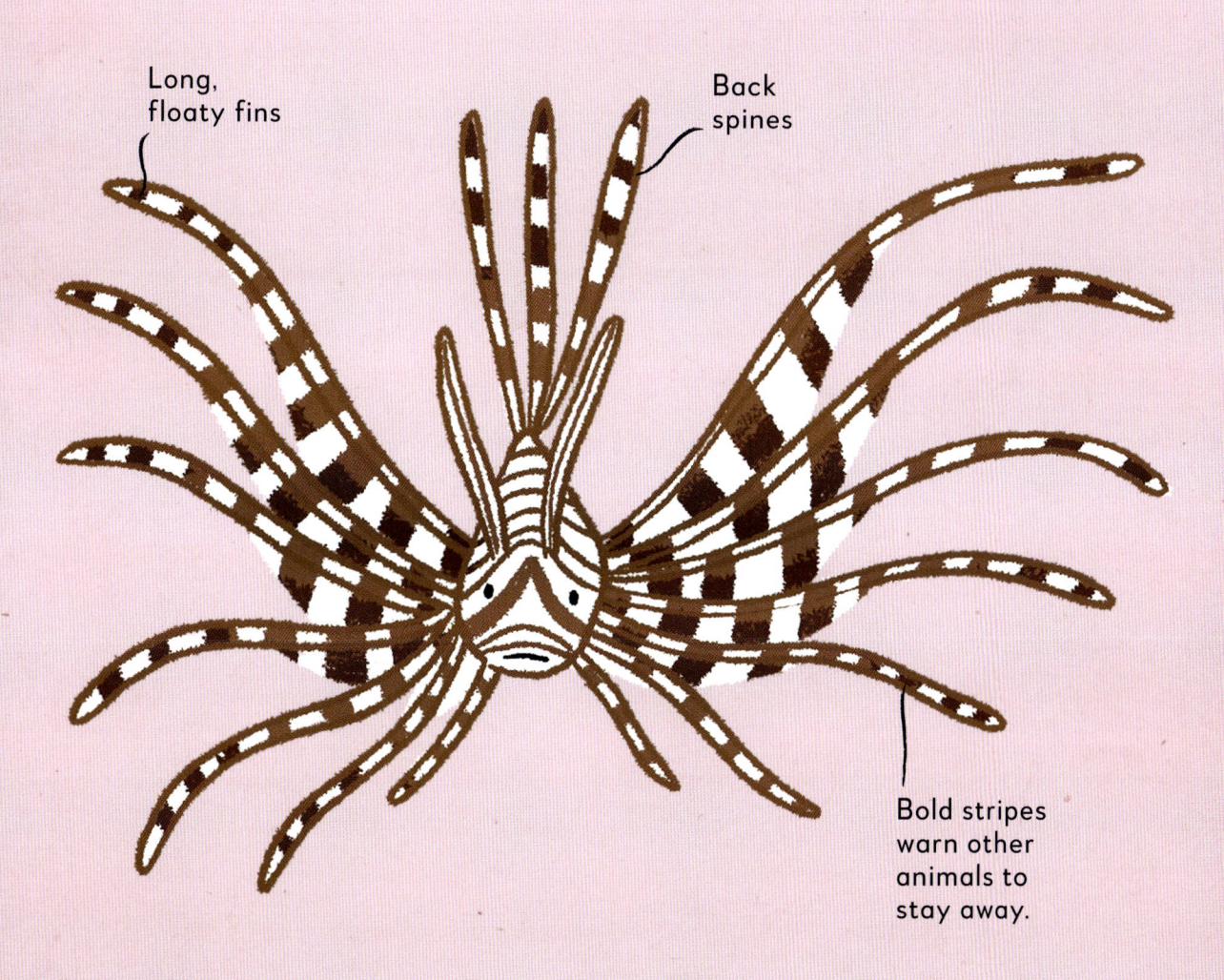

Long, floaty fins

Back spines

Bold stripes warn other animals to stay away.

Fish

Seahorse

Seahorses live in shallow sea waters. They swim **upright** and use their back fin to push themselves through the water.

Seahorses **wrap** their curly tails around corals and seaweed to keep from floating away.

The head is shaped like a horse's.

Baby seahorses are called fry.

Tiny, spiny plates cover the entire body.

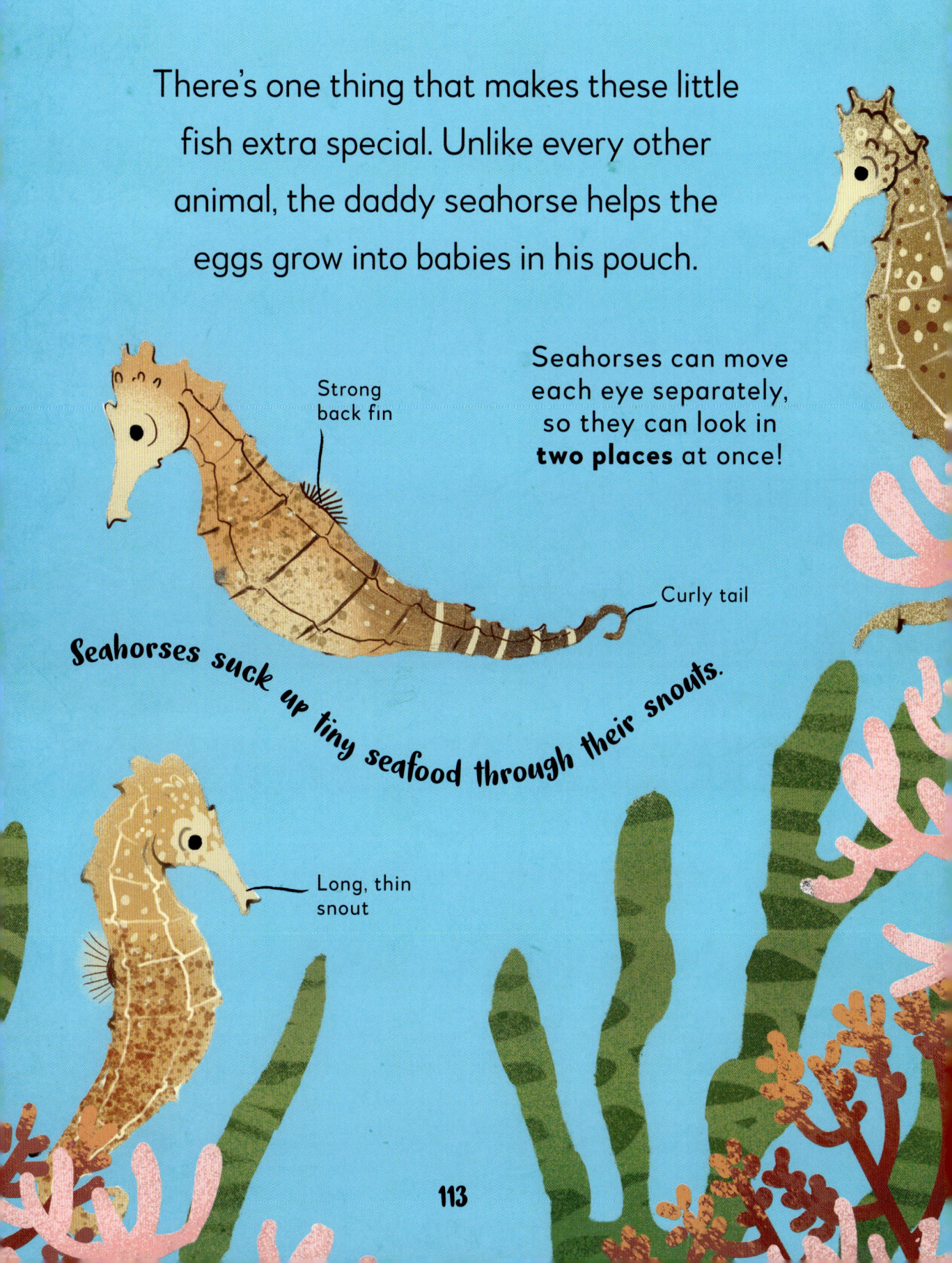

There's one thing that makes these little fish extra special. Unlike every other animal, the daddy seahorse helps the eggs grow into babies in his pouch.

Strong back fin

Seahorses can move each eye separately, so they can look in **two places** at once!

Curly tail

Seahorses suck up tiny seafood through their snouts.

Long, thin snout

Fish

X-ray fish live in large groups called shoals.

Stripy fins   Bony skeleton

X-ray fish

X-ray fish are almost transparent. You can look right through their **shimmering** scales and see the shape of their backbone and skeleton.

Piranha

Piranhas live in groups in rivers and streams. They have **razor-sharp** teeth that they use to eat insects, other fish, worms, and plants.

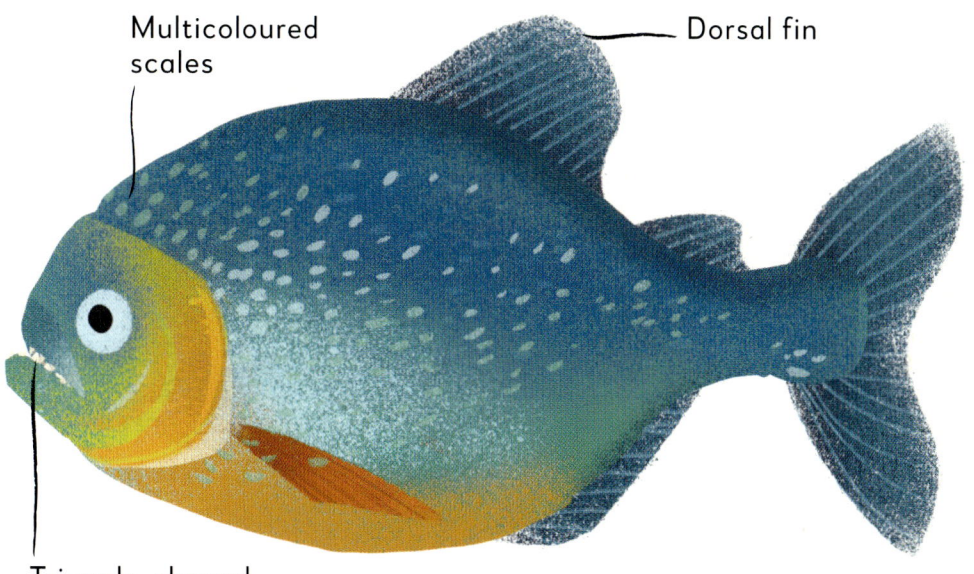

Multicoloured scales

Dorsal fin

Triangle-shaped teeth

Piranhas grow several sets of teeth in their lifetime.

Fish

Stingray

These disc-shaped creatures use their fins to glide through the water. Stingrays have venomous spikes called **barbs** on their tails, which help them to fight off predators.

Wing-like fins

Long, thin tail

A large group of stingrays is called a fever.

Eyes on top of the body

Dorsal fin

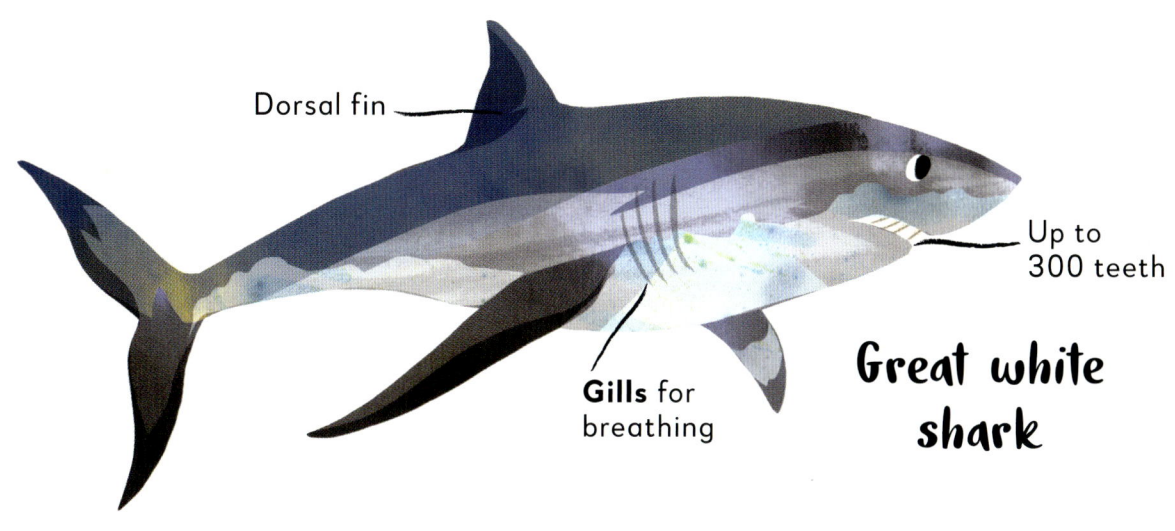

Up to 300 teeth

Gills for breathing

Great white shark

Shark

There are hundreds of different sharks in the oceans. Many sharks have lots of sharp teeth that they use to **attack** other fish. Their smooth bodies and powerful fins help them swim fast.

Tiny animals get caught in the shark's wide-open **mouth**.

Basking shark

This **gentle** shark does not have big teeth.

Invertebrates

Invertebrates don't have bones, which means they can be squishy, like a slug. However, they can also be spiky, strong, and often strange in interesting ways!

Invertebrates

Spiky body spines protect from hungry predators.

Round body shape

Sea urchin

Sea urchins are round and spiky. They move slowly across the seabed eating any seaweed in their path. Underneath their sharp spines is a hard **shell**.

Sea urchins live by rocks and seaweed.

These creatures often live in groups called herds.

Starfish

Starfish live on the **seabed**. They move around using thousands of tiny feet, which are found under each of their **five** arms.

Spotty orange skin

There is an eye at the end of each arm.

Starfish

Starfish and brittle stars do not have brains.

Round body

The thin arms snap off easily.

Brittle stars are like starfish, but have **thinner** arms.

Brittle star

Invertebrates

Flying insects

Believe it or not, these tiny insects are super strong. They need to be, because they beat their wings so hard to stay in the air. That's what makes them **buzz**.

Large eyes

Fly

Flying ants are like normal ants but with wings!

All insects have six legs.

Flying ant

Fuzzy body hair

Bumblebee

These **bees** fly to flowers to drink the **nectar** inside.

Two thin antennae

Antennae help insects to detect what is around them.

Long legs

Praying mantis

Lacy pattern on wings

Green lacewing

Slender waist

Wasp

Wasps have stingers at the end of their bodies.

There are millions of types of flying insects. Some have a nasty **sting** to defend themselves!

Invertebrates

Butterfly

A butterfly starts out life as a **caterpillar**. This tiny bug chomps on leaves, then begins to change form. First it becomes a **chrysalis**, before turning into a fluttering butterfly.

Soft, squishy body

Patterned skin

Caterpillar

Butterflies drink sweet **nectar** from plants and flowers. They have wings with beautiful patterns and can fly.

Two wings on each side

Long antennae for balance and smell

Butterfly

Dragonfly

Dragonflies are buzzing, acrobatic hunters that can catch flying prey in mid-air. They can zoom straight up and down or **hover** in one place like a helicopter.

Four wings

Tiny head

Long, thin tail

Invertebrates

Beetle

These insects come in all kinds of colours and live in almost every part of the world. They are some of nature's best **cleaners**, because many of them eat up dead plants and animals.

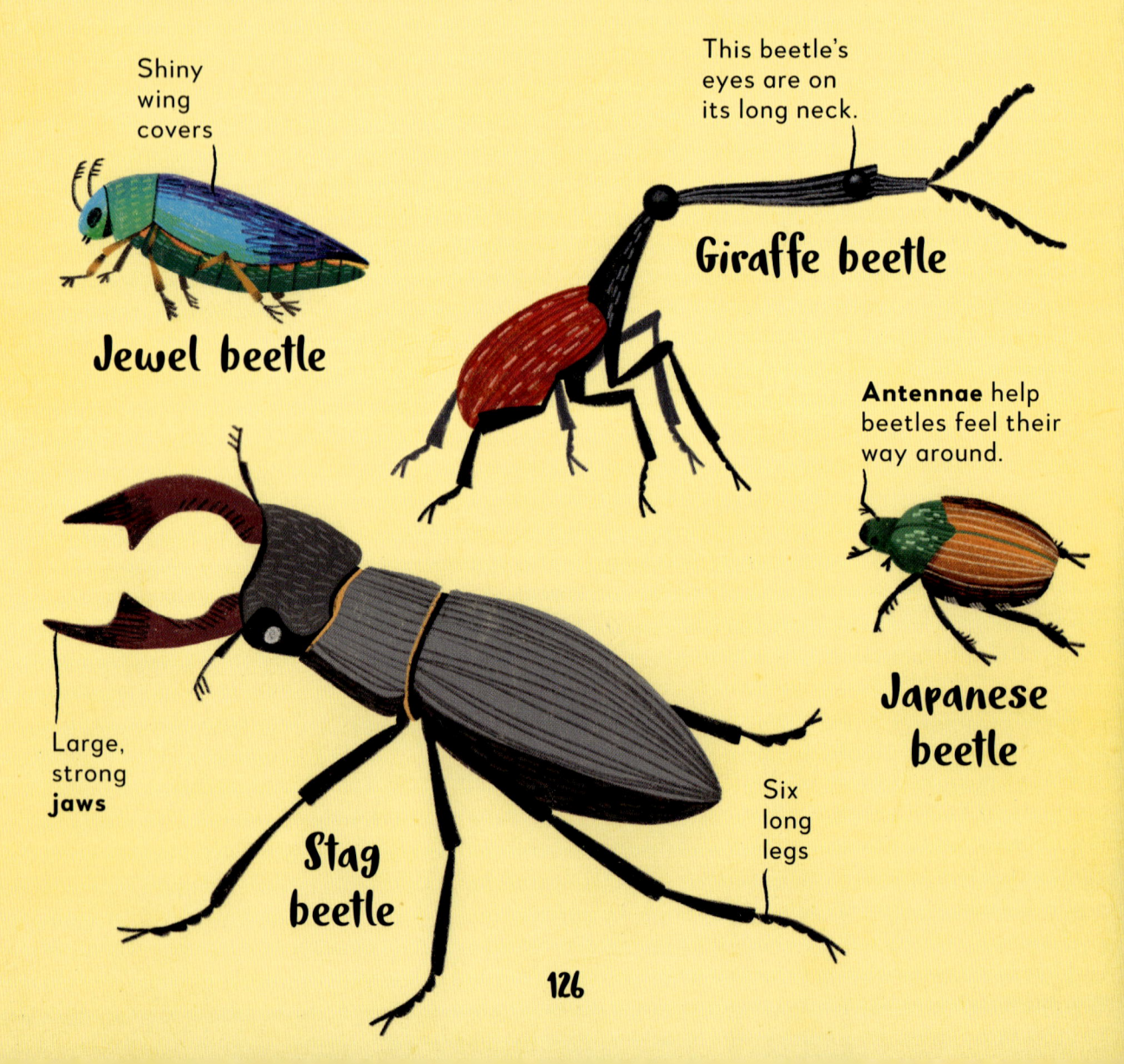

Shiny wing covers

This beetle's eyes are on its long neck.

Jewel beetle

Giraffe beetle

Antennae help beetles feel their way around.

Japanese beetle

Large, strong **jaws**

Six long legs

Stag beetle

22-spot ladybird

Orange ladybird

A ladybird's **spots** warn other animals to stay away.

Six short legs

Wings are hidden under wing covers.

Two-spot ladybird

Seven-spot ladybird

Two tiny eyes

Ladybird

Cream-spot ladybird

Ladybirds are beetles. There are thousands of different types. Some have **no spots**, while others are covered in them.

Invertebrates

Scorpion

Scorpions are small but mighty. They have eight legs and two large pincers. At the end of their tail is a **venomous** stinger.

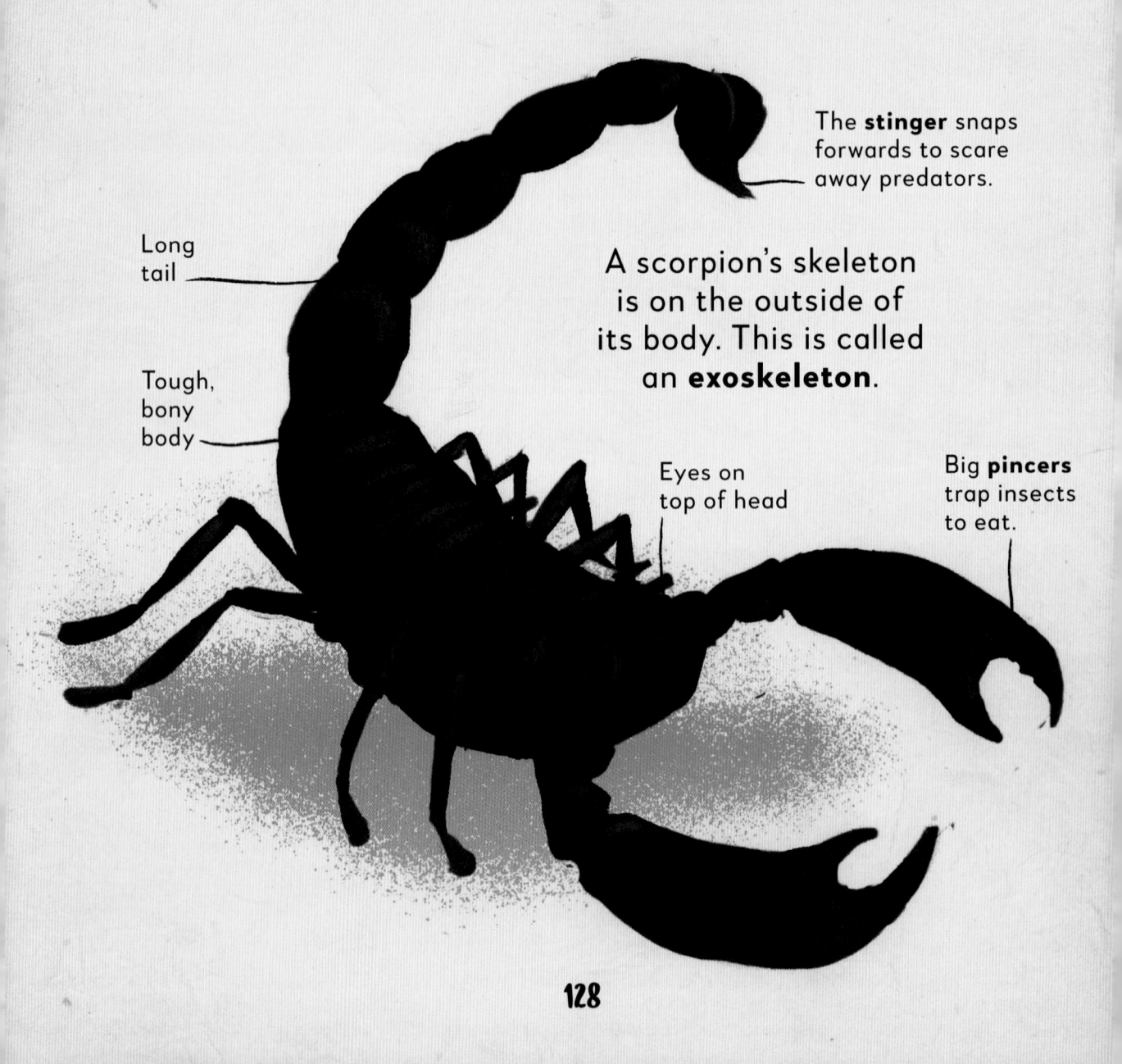

The **stinger** snaps forwards to scare away predators.

Long tail

A scorpion's skeleton is on the outside of its body. This is called an **exoskeleton**.

Tough, bony body

Eyes on top of head

Big **pincers** trap insects to eat.

Spider

Spiders come in many different shapes, sizes, and colours. They all have eight legs, many have eight eyes, and some **spin** sticky webs.

Many spiders make silk to create webs.

Marbled orb-weaver

Long front legs catch food.

Crab spider

Red-orange legs

Mexican red knee tarantula

Invertebrates

Crab

Crabs can live on land or in the sea. They use their back legs to **scuttle** sideways on sand. Their two front legs have claws on each end for grabbing food.

Crabs are protected from predators by a hard shell.

Orange shell

Ten legs

Large claws on the two front legs

Mantis shrimp

Mantis shrimp pack a fast **punch**! If another animal gets too close, they use their front legs to thump it.

Bright green shell

Two huge eyes

Mantis shrimp keep their front legs tucked away when not using them.

Krill

Almost see-through body

Krill live together in huge groups, called swarms. Many krill can flash **lights** from their bodies to scare away predators.

Tiny legs

Two beady eyes

Invertebrates

When scared, octopuses squirt out ink.

An octopus has **nine brains** and **three hearts**.

Large head

Spotty skin

Eight wiggly arms

Octopus

Wriggling, muscly octopuses swim through the water powered by their eight arms. Each arm has hundreds of sticky **suckers** that help the octopus to move around and to grab prey.

Cuttlefish

This cunning creature would be great at hide-and-seek. It can **change** colour to look like rocks or sand on the seabed!

Long, flappy fin

These soft-bodied invertebrates are all types of mollusc.

Nautilus

The nautilus has almost one hundred arms, called **tentacles**. It stretches them out of its hard shell to catch food.

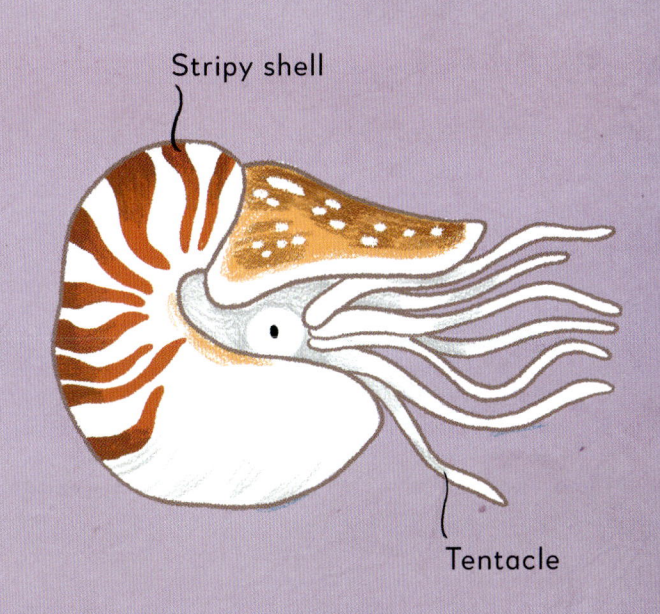

Stripy shell

Tentacle

Invertebrates

All these animals are molluscs, too.

Snail

Snails can pull their bodies into their hard shells. They make **slime**, which they slide around on to move.

Spiral shell

Two antennae help slugs feel what is around them.

Slug

Slugs crawl by making wave movements with their **foot**. They live in damp places.

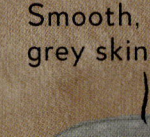

Foot

Smooth, grey skin

Mussel

Each mussel is surrounded by two hard shells.

Mussels live on sea shores. They **suck** in water to take tiny food out of it.

Nudibranch

These colourful sea slugs live on the **seabed**. They breathe through their skin or feathery gills.

Gills on back

Spotty, bumpy skin

Smooth, stripy skin

Invertebrates

A jellyfish's body is called a **bell**.

Jellyfish

Squishy jellyfish have no brain, heart, bones, or eyes. They **drift** along with ocean currents.

Arms with stingers

Sea pens **glow** in the dark when touched.

Branches of tentacles

Sea pen

Sea pens live on the seabed. They use their tentacles to catch food that is **floating** nearby.

Long stem

Anemone

Anemones live in **shallow** sea waters. They are not rooted in place, and can move across the seabed.

Tentacles hide an anemone's mouth.

Coral

Tropical waters are filled with beautiful groups of corals. These animals can form huge mounds called **reefs**.

Sticky tentacles for catching food

Extinct

Here are some of the many animals that once lived on Earth, but sadly no longer exist.

Triceratops was a plant-eating **dinosaur** with three long horns. It lived millions of years ago.

Horn

Thick tail

Triceratops

Curling **tusks**

Long **trunk**

This elephant-sized beast lived in ice-cold lands **thousands** of years ago. Mammoths were hunted by ancient humans.

Woolly mammoth

These **birds** were about the size of a turkey. Humans hunted them, and the last dodo was seen in 1662.

Dodo

Large beak

Clawed feet

Endangered

There are only a small number of these animals left. They may become extinct very soon.

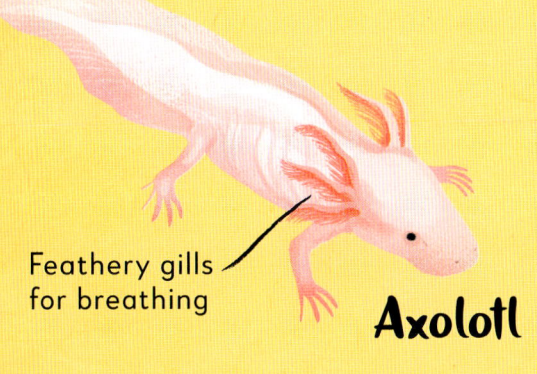

Axolotls now live in just a few lakes. **Dirty water** from a nearby city has made it hard for them to survive.

Feathery gills for breathing

Axolotl

No back fin

These porpoises are unusual because they live in a river. Many get caught in **fishing nets** by accident.

Yangtze finless porpoise

Horn

Javan rhinoceros

This is one of the **rarest** animals on Earth. There are only around 60 left. Each one has been given a name, to help us track and protect them.

Glossary

armour
Protective covering on an animal that keeps it from being harmed

backbone
Spine of an animal

blend
When an animal can match its surroundings

burrow
To dig down into the ground, or the hole where an animal lives

chrysalis
Stage of growth from caterpillar to butterfly

desert
Hot or cold place where not much rain falls

dorsal fin
Fin on the back of fish and marine mammals used for balance when swimming

grassland
Wide-open space covered by grass and flowers

habitat
Best place for specific animals to live. For example, sharks live in ocean habitats

lagoon
Area of shallow pond-like water

mollusc
Type of invertebrate with a soft body and, often, a hard shell

nectar
Sugary sweet liquid from a flower

nocturnal
Animals that sleep during the day and are awake at night-time

poisonous
If something is poisonous, it contains poison – a substance that kills or damages living things

predator
Animal that hunts other animals

prey
Animal that is hunted by another animal

rainforest
Area with many trees where there is a large amount of rain

savannah
Large area of flat land with few trees, found in hot places

senses
Animal's view of the world using the five senses: sight, smell, taste, hearing, and touch

sensitive
When an animal can sense tiny things using its sense of touch

skeleton
Bony structure of an animal's body

transparent
See-through

tropical
Weather or habitat that is hot and damp

venom
Poisonous liquid

venomous
Animal that is able to pass on venom through a bite or sting

waterproof
Something that does not let water in. For example, skin is waterproof

wetland
Area of wet, muddy land where plants grow

wild
Where an animal lives free in the world

Animal A-Z

Aa
alligators 93
alpacas 40
ants 122
anteaters 60–61
armadillos 61
axolotls 139

Bb
badgers 23
bats 48–49
beavers 55
bees 122
beetles 9, 126–127
black panthers 15
bobcats 13
brown bears 26
buffalo 36
butterflies 124

Cc
caimans 93
camels 38
capybaras 54
caterpillars 124
cats 16–17
chameleons 96–97
cheetahs 13
chickens 87
cockatoos 73
condors 78
corals 137

cows 37
crabs 130
crocodiles 92
cuttlefish 133

Dd
deer 35
dingoes 21
dinosaurs 138
dodos 138
dogs 18–19
dolphins 44
dragonflies 125
ducks 85

Ee
eagles 79
echidnas 67
elephants 62–63

Ff
flamingoes 84
flies 122
foxes 21
frogs 105

Gg
geese 85
giant pandas 28
giraffes 39
gorillas 56
green lacewings 123
guinea pigs 55

Hh
hares 53
hedgehogs 50
hippopotamuses 46–47
horses 32

Ii
iguanas 95

Jj
jaguars 15
jellyfish 136

Kk
kangaroos 64
kingfishers 76
kiwis 88
koalas 64
kookaburras 77
krill 131

Ll
ladybirds 127
leopards 14
lionfish 111
lions 9, 12
lizards 94–97
llamas 41

Mm
mantis shrimps 131
mice 54
moles 51

monkeys 58–59
moose.......................... 35
mussels 135

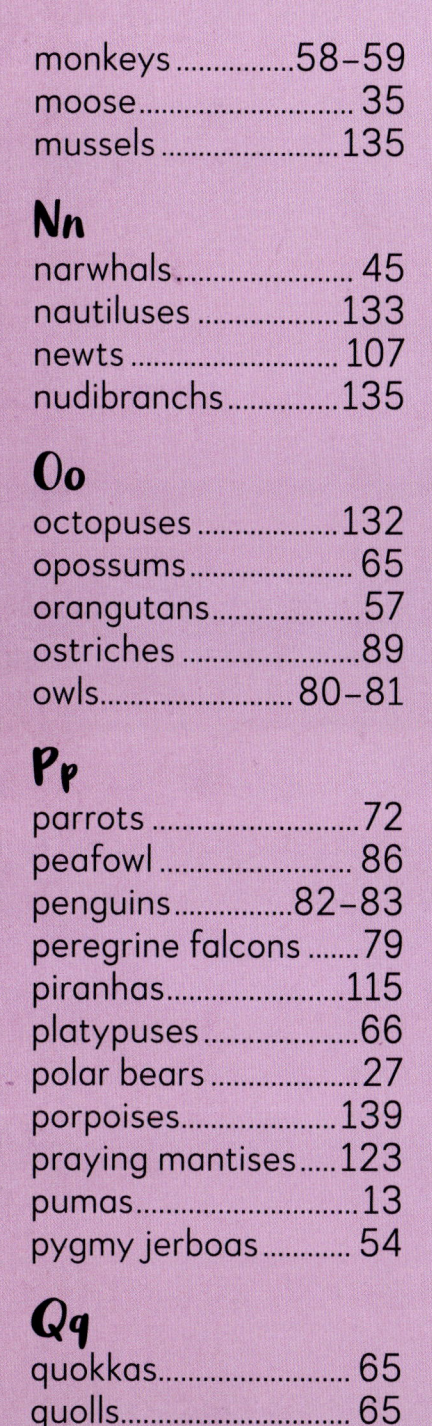

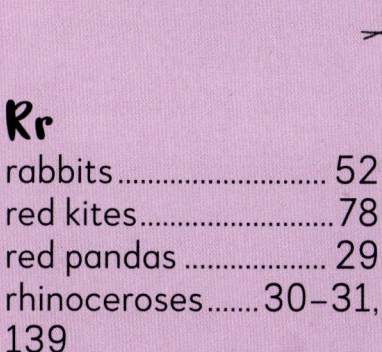

Nn
narwhals...................... 45
nautiluses 133
newts 107
nudibranchs...............135

Oo
octopuses 132
opossums 65
orangutans.................. 57
ostriches 89
owls......................80–81

Pp
parrots 72
peafowl 86
penguins...............82–83
peregrine falcons 79
piranhas....................115
platypuses.................. 66
polar bears 27
porpoises..................139
praying mantises.....123
pumas......................... 13
pygmy jerboas 54

Qq
quokkas...................... 65
quolls.......................... 65

Rr
rabbits 52
red kites..................... 78
red pandas 29
rhinoceroses.......30–31, 139

Ss
salamanders.............106
scorpions...................128
sea otters...................22
sea pens 136
sea turtles 100
sea urchins 120
seahorses..........112–113
seals 25
sharks.......................117
sheep 37
skunks....................... 23
sloths 60
slugs 134
snails 134
snakes 98–99
snow leopards 14
songbirds 70–71
spiders......................129
starfish 121
stingrays 116
swans......................... 85

Tt
tigers.......................... 12
toads 104
tortoises 101
toucans 74

Vv
vicuñas....................... 41
vultures...................... 79

Ww
wallabies.................... 65
walruses..................... 24
wasps.......................123
whales 42–43
wolves........................ 20
wombats.................... 64
woodpeckers 75
woolly mammoths...138

Xx
X-ray fish 114

Yy
yaks............................ 34

Zz
zebrafish...................110
zebras........................ 33

Author Zeshan Akhter
Illustrators Jean Claude, Livi Gosling, Kaja Kajfez, Charlotte Milner, Marc Pattenden, Sandhya Prabhat, Kate Slater, Sara Ugolotti

Editor Katie Lawrence
Designer Sonny Flynn
Senior designer and jacket designer Elle Ward
Editorial assistant Kieran Jones
Design assistants Sif Nørskov, Holly Price
Publishing coordinator Issy Walsh
Managing editor Jonathan Melmoth
Managing art editor Diane Peyton Jones
Production editor Dragana Puvacic
Production controller Magdalena Bojko
Deputy art director Mabel Chan
Publishing director Sarah Larter

Educational consultant Penny Coltman

This edition published in 2024
First published in Great Britain in 2022 by
Dorling Kindersley Limited
DK, One Embassy Gardens, 8 Viaduct Gardens,
London SW11 7BW

The authorised representative in the EEA is
Dorling Kindersley Verlag GmbH. Arnulfstr. 124,
80636 Munich, Germany

Copyright © 2024 Dorling Kindersley Limited
A Penguin Random House Company
10 9 8 7 6 5 4 3 2
002–340599–Aug/2024

All rights reserved.
No part of this publication may be reproduced, stored in or introduced into a retrieval system, or transmitted, in any form, or by any means (electronic, mechanical, photocopying, recording, or otherwise), without the prior written permission of the copyright owner.

A CIP catalogue record for this book
is available from the British Library.
ISBN: 978-0-2416-6989-1

Printed and bound in China

www.dk.com

Acknowledgements

DK would like to thank: Helen Peters for the index and Caroline Hunt for proofreading.

Illustrations copyright © Charlotte Milner 2018:
11 Brown bear. **26** Brown bear. **122** Bumblebee.
Cover Bumblebee.

Illustrations copyright © Sandhya Prabhat 2020:
69 Parrot. **73** Cockatoo. **72** Parrots. **91** Blue iguana. **95** Iguanas. **Cover** Parrots.

Illustrations copyright © Kate Slater 2020:
18–19 Dogs. **39** Giraffe. **52** Rabbit. **60–61** Anteater. **62–63** Elephants. **78** Andean condor, Red kite. **79** King vulture. **122** Fly, Flying ant. **Cover** Dog, Giraffe.

Illustrations copyright © Kate Slater 2022:
4–5 Tree of Life. **11** Mouse. **27** Polar bear. **53** Hares. **54–55** Rodents. **60–61** Sloth, Armadillo. **69** Bald eagle. **70–71** Songbirds. **79** Bald eagle, Peregrine falcon. **84** Flamingos. **85** Swans, Goose, Ducks. **109** Great white shark. **117** Sharks. **118** Praying mantis. **123** Praying mantis, Green lacewing, Wasp. **Cover** Flamingos.

Picture credits
1–144 123RF.com: laurent davoust
for background texture

All other images © Dorling Kindersley

This book was made with Forest Stewardship Council™ certified paper – one small step in DK's commitment to a sustainable future. Learn more at www.dk.com/uk/information/sustainability